HORRIBLE SCIENCE

SUFFERING SCIENTISTS

NICK ARNOLD

D0980663

Illustrated by
Tony De Saulles

Hippo

Scholastic Children's Books,
Commonwealth House, 1-19 New Oxford Street
London WC1A 1NU, UK

A division of Scholastic Ltd
London ~ New York ~ Toronto ~ Sydney ~ Auckland
Mexico City ~ New Delhi ~ Hong Kong

First published in the UK by Scholastic Ltd, 2000

Text copyright © Nick Arnold, 2000
Illustrations copyright © Tony De Saulles, 2000

ISBN 0 439 01211 2

Typeset by Falcon Oast Graphic Art, East Hoathly, Sussex
Printed and bound by Bath Press, Bath.

10 9 8 7 6 5 4 3 2

The right of Nick Arnold and Tony De Saulles to be identified as the author and
illustrator of this work respectively has been asserted by them in accordance with
the Copyright, Designs and Patents Act, 1988.

Contents

Nick Arnold has been writing stories and books since he was a youngster, but never dreamt he'd find fame writing about suffering scientists. His research involved meeting scientists, trying on their lab coats and undergoing their experiments and he enjoyed every minute of it.

When he's not delving into Horrible Science, his hobbies include eating pizza, riding his bike and thinking up corny jokes (though not all at the same time).

Tony De Saulles picked up his crayons when he was still in nappies and has been doodling ever since. He takes Horrible Science very seriously and even agreed to sketch experiments that went explosively wrong. Fortunately, he has made a full recovery.

When he's not out with his sketchpad, Tony likes to write poetry and play squash, though he hasn't written any poetry about squash yet.

INTRODUCTION

Another day, another science lesson. As you listen to the quiet boring drone of your teacher's voice you begin to feel sleepy. The room is nice and warm and before you know it you're fast asleep. Asleep and dreaming...

Dreaming that YOU are a famous scientist.

And then you wake up with a jolt...

The dream gets you thinking. Is it really worth becoming a scientist? Well, on the plus side there's the glory and fame and excitement of making a great discovery...

The minus side...
Science is horrible, and just as you suffer in science lessons, so scientists suffer for science. Did you know there was a scientist who had his head cut off, and that some scientists were poisoned by the chemicals they discovered, and that one scientist jumped into a volcano? So, should *you* risk becoming a scientist? Or is it too *dangerous*?

Well, before you make up your mind, maybe you ought to read about suffering scientists. Of course, you won't read the all-important stomach-churning details in any old science book. What you need is a HORRIBLE science book full of gruesome facts to tell you the horrible truth about Science. But hold on ... looks like you've found one. And you're already reading it! Oh well, don't let me stop you...

HORRIBLE HEALTH WARNING!

DISGUSTING DETAILS AHEAD

PART ONE

SUFFERING
ANCIENT
SCIENTISTS

SCIENCE STARTS HERE

Before you decide whether to be a scientist you need to know what science is and where it came from. Oh – so you think you know all that? Well, if someone asked you,

how would you reply?

a) A boring lesson that I can't keep awake in.

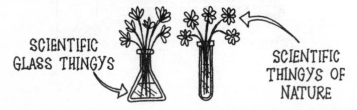

b) Something done by bods in white coats who can't speak plain English.

ESSENTIALLY, THE ALBUMEN AND YOLK ARE SUBMERGED IN H₂0, WHICH VAPORIZES AT 100°F, AND LEFT FOR 240 SECONDS

(HE'S BOILING AN EGG)

c) Something to do with test-tubes and drawing flowers.

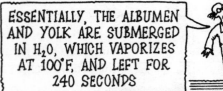

SCIENTIFIC GLASS THINGYS

SCIENTIFIC THINGYS OF NATURE

Whilst there might be grains of truth in all of these answers, none of them really sum up the essence of what science is about. So if you said **a)**, **b)** OR **c)** you'd better read on...

Suffering scientists fact file

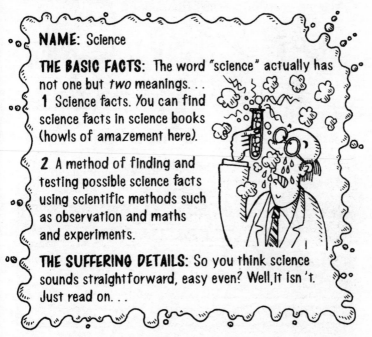

NAME: Science

THE BASIC FACTS: The word "science" actually has not one but *two* meanings...

1 Science facts. You can find science facts in science books (howls of amazement here).

2 A method of finding and testing possible science facts using scientific methods such as observation and maths and experiments.

THE SUFFERING DETAILS: So you think science sounds straightforward, easy even? Well, it isn't. Just read on...

Let's imagine you actually were a scientist and you thought up a brilliant science idea whilst sitting on the toilet. (Of course, you'd be flushed with success.)

EUREKA!

No way.

9

You didn't think that being a scientist was that *easy*, did you?

To prove that your great idea is a genuine scientific fact and not just a flush in the pan (oh dear, we're back to toilets again), you have to use those boring old scientific methods.

And these might involve...

• Making years of patient observations.

• Struggling with horribly complicated mathematics to come up with a formula that explains your discovery.

• And undertaking endless experiments.

And you thought *you* had it tough...

Suffering expressions

I WAS LOOKING FOR A LAW BUT MY HYPOTHESIS ISN'T RIGHT

Should you call an ambulance?

Answer: No. A hypothesis (hi-poth-thiss-sis) is the posh term for a scientific idea that hasn't been proved to be wrong yet. A law is a fact that has been agreed to be true. Several laws can be put together to make a theory which scientists use to explain the world. Got all that?

But where did scientific methods come from? Surely there must have been a time before there were scientists.

A happy thought

Once upon a time, a long time ago (say 20,000 years before you were born), there was no such thing as science, so no scientists, no experiments and definitely no science lessons. Wow! Isn't that a happy thought?

DRONE, WITTER, PHYSICS, BLAH, BLAH, MUMBLE, CHEMISTRY, MUTTER, BIOLOGY

YES!

In those days people were just as curious about their surroundings as the average two-year-old is today. And they made lots of discoveries. Like fire. Early humans probably got fire from volcanoes, and they soon found fire was a hot idea for cooking and heating and making chewy mammoth steak a bit less rubbery. Then they learnt how to make fire by rubbing sticks together. Of course, because scientific methods hadn't been invented yet these discoveries were made by trial and error … as we're about to find out. Let's take a look at an average Stone Age family. Meet the Ugs...

THE UGS. . . A VERY BRIGHT IDEA

WHAT WE NEED IS A BIT OF EXTRA LIGHT.

SOUNDS LIKE A BRIGHT IDEA!

HMMM, MAMMOTH FAT BURNS WELL, SO WHAT HAPPENS IF I PUT SOME FAT IN THIS CLAY POT?

LET'S TRY STICKING SOME WOOD IN THE FAT. I RECKON THE WOOD WILL SOAK UP THE HOT FAT AND BURN WITH A NICE FLAME

YOU'RE A GENIUS, MUM!

IT'S JUST OLD-FASHIONED TRIAL AND ERROR

By about 5,000 BC important people were asking deep meaningful questions like "where did we come from?" –

the sort of things that scientists would also later want to know. These people were priests. But we're not talking about your local friendly vicar. In those days, in ancient towns all over the world, priests were powerful people who advised kings and worked in temples.

ANCIENT PRIEST FROM LONG AGO

FRIENDLY VICAR OF TODAY

They often sacrificed animals to the gods, and in times of crisis priests in Central America and the Middle East usually killed the odd child. So if your neighbourhood priest came round clutching a huge knife and muttering about "little sacrifices", he wasn't collecting for the church roof fund. The priests thought killing children was the only way to keep the gods happy. In those days, priests thought their gods caused everything. Take lightning, for example.

DON'T WORRY – IT'S ONLY THE GODS THROWING THUNDERBOLTS

But even in those days there were people who were thinking a bit more like modern scientists. There were gifted mathematicians in ancient Egypt and the Middle East and China from about 2,500 BC and they all had one thing in common. They had to make accurate calculations for which there was only one right answer. (This fact can be a real problem for children in maths tests.)

Of course, scientists make calculations too.

The first people to try to explain things in terms of natural forces and not gods lived in ancient Greece and China. We'll go to Greece in a minute but first let's take a quick trip to China where lots of amazing discoveries were made. Trouble is that people in the rest of the world didn't get to hear about many of them.

But you can – simply by reading on.

THE SUFFERING CHINESE

For hundreds of years people in China were making discoveries that would have gob-smacked the average European at the time. Ancient Chinese inventors came up with, amongst other things, kites (390 BC) and wheelbarrows (AD 400). But life wasn't all plain sailing for Chinese thinkers and inventors, as you're about to find out…

> INCREDIBLE!.., WHAT THE HECK ARE THEY?

China: the bad news for Science

Since ancient times, China had been ruled by a succession of emperors who could do exactly what they wanted – they were that powerful. According to legend, in ancient times an eclipse of the sun (that's when the sun is hidden behind the moon) happened unexpectedly. The two royal astronomers at the time, Hsi and Ho, had failed to predict the eclipse. So their emperor had them executed.

> I PREDICT THAT NEITHER OF YOU WILL SEE THE SUN AGAIN. . . EVER!

Another emperor, Emperor Shih Huang Ti (259-210 BC) didn't like old books. In 212 BC he decided to have them all burnt so that any dangerous knowledge that could be used

15

against him would be lost. China's ancient scientific knowledge went up in flames. Oh well, that must be the ultimate excuse for not doing homework.

And brutal emperors weren't the only difficulties faced by China's thinkers.

- China is a big country and ideas didn't spread far outside a small group of highly educated people.
- Travelling from Europe to China was difficult. You couldn't just hop on a jet for Beijing. You had to ride for months on the back of a smelly camel across bandit-infested deserts and mountains. So it was quite hard for news of discoveries to spread between China and Europe.

- The writers of Chinese history books were more interested in recording the glorious deeds of the emperors than the names of often humble people who made discoveries. So, many gifted Chinese people are simply forgotten. Some great Chinese inventor must have invented a way of smoking out houses to get rid of bugs (600 BC – I expect they were puffed with success), or making porcelain (around AD 700 – a real cracking discovery) or farming silkworm caterpillars to make silk (2,600 BC – they must have been a smooth operator), but no one knows *who*.

Test your teacher

a) 1922
b) 1743
c) First century BC

Answer: c) They built drill rigs from bamboo with cast iron drill tips that bored through the rock at a rather slow 2.54 cm (1 inch) a day (that really is boring!) and reached depths of 1,400 metres (4,800 feet). The Chinese engineers were searching for salty water to make salt from. But sometimes they hit gas so they used it to boil up the salty water in order to evaporate the water and leave salt behind.

Ingenious Heng

Sadly, as usual, no one knows the names of these ingenious engineers. But here's one great Chinese scientist who is still remembered: astronomer Heng Zhang (AD 78-139).

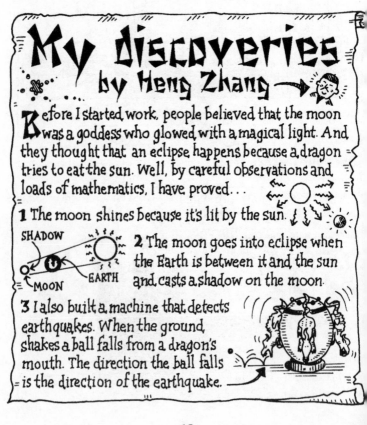

My discoveries
by Heng Zhang →

Before I started work, people believed that the moon was a goddess who glowed with a magical light. And they thought that an eclipse happens because a dragon tries to eat the sun. Well, by careful observations and loads of mathematics, I have proved...

1 The moon shines because it's lit by the sun.

SHADOW

2 The moon goes into eclipse when the Earth is between it and the sun and casts a shadow on the moon.

MOON EARTH

3 I also built a machine that detects earthquakes. When the ground shakes a ball falls from a dragon's mouth. The direction the ball falls is the direction of the earthquake.

Bet you never knew!
One major Chinese discovery was gunpowder. This seems to have been invented around AD 250 and was used for fireworks and weapons to scare enemy horses. But surprise, surprise – we don't know who made this brilliant breakthrough. Whoever they were, they were sure to have been blown away by their discovery.

SPOT THE INVENTOR COMPETITION

Meanwhile, back in Europe, a separate tradition of science that would one day lead to rockets to the moon and frozen fish fingers was developing. It had been kicked off by a mysterious and little-known genius. Wanna know who he was?

Well, read on and find out...

I WILL... AFTER I'VE COOKED THESE FISH FINGERS

19

TALENTED THALES

The ancient Greeks were a really jumping, jiving happening kind of people – completely buzzing with ideas. They were thinkers, writers and early scientists – all busy dreaming up new theories to explain what made the world tick. And one of the most talented Greeks was Thales of Miletus, who lived in a Greek city in what is now Turkey.

Horrible Science Hall of Fame: Thales
(625-547 BC) NATIONALITY: Greek

Thales is reckoned to be the first known person ever to explain things as a modern scientist would in terms of natural causes and effects rather than in terms of religion like a priest. One day Thales rubbed a piece of amber and found that it attracted things to it by a mysterious force that we now call static electricity. The amber can even give you a shock if you touch it accidentally.

THE GODS ARE ANGRY!

YOU SAY THAT ABOUT EVERYTHING YOU DON'T UNDERSTAND!

NOW HE'S ANGRY

No one knows if Thales was the first person to get such a shock. But he was certainly the first person to believe that it had natural causes ... like rubbing amber ... and no divine ones.

Thales must have been a very busy person.

- According to one story he visited Egypt and learnt geometry from the local priests. (Geometry is the branch of maths that deals with shapes.) He was the first person to teach the subject to the Greeks. Lucky Greeks, I don't think. But that wasn't all. Thales was also...
- A politician who advised on the setting up of a local parliament.
- A merchant who used his scientific knowledge to make money. He used a lodestone (a natural magnetic stone that pointed north) to guide his ships.

Bet you never knew!

According to another story, Thales' neighbours teased him about his scientific interests:

But Thales used his knowledge to forecast a good olive crop. He bought up all the olive presses that were used to make olive oil and made pots of money.

Water Blunder

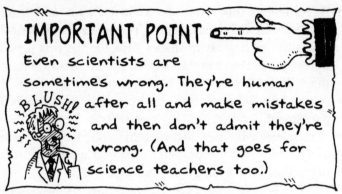

IMPORTANT POINT

Even scientists are sometimes wrong. They're human after all and make mistakes and then don't admit they're wrong. (And that goes for science teachers too.)

BLUSH!

Well, you can rely on this book to tell you how scientists made their biggest blunders. Here's Thales' biggest ever slip-up.

Thales reckoned the Earth was floating in water. When the water gets a bit choppy you get earthquakes.

I CAN'T STOP SHAKING!

IT'S JUST SEA-SICKNESS

Wrong – but not completely. Scientists now know that the surface of the Earth that we walk on is made up of vast plates of rock thousands of kilometres across that float on a layer of melted rock beneath. (I suppose that's what you call rock'n'roll.) But at least Thales was trying to think logically about why certain things happen.

More suffering Greeks

In ancient Greece there were many rich, well-educated people who didn't have to work for a living and had slaves to peel their grapes and cut their toe nails. Wouldn't it be great to have your own slave? You could even send your slave to school in your place. With so little to do, some of the smarter ancient Greeks used their time thinking up new ideas. And a few began to have scientific ideas...

Democritus (460-380 BC) reckoned that atoms were the smallest objects in the universe. But he didn't perform any experiments to show that they existed. He simply thought it was logical to believe there must be something too small for you to cut in half.

Suffering scientists fact file

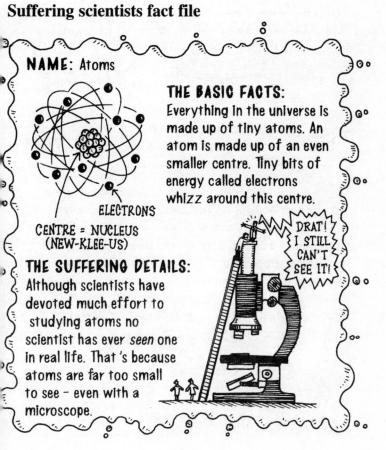

NAME: Atoms

ELECTRONS

CENTRE = NUCLEUS
(NEW-KLEE-US)

THE BASIC FACTS:
Everything in the universe is made up of tiny atoms. An atom is made up of an even smaller centre. Tiny bits of energy called electrons whizz around this centre.

THE SUFFERING DETAILS:
Although scientists have devoted much effort to studying atoms no scientist has ever *seen* one in real life. That's because atoms are far too small to see – even with a microscope.

DRAT! I STILL CAN'T SEE IT!

Eratosthenes (276-194 BC) worked in Alexandria, Egypt as a librarian. His greatest achievement was to calculate the size of the Earth by measuring differences in the sun's angle at midday in two different locations in Egypt. The difference was due to the curve of the Earth's surface and to complete his calculation, Eratosthenes ordered a slave to walk the distance, about 820 km (500 miles), between the two towns Alexandria and Syene, and to *count every single step*. Maths did the rest. Eratosthenes became famous for ever and his slave probably got a nasty blister.

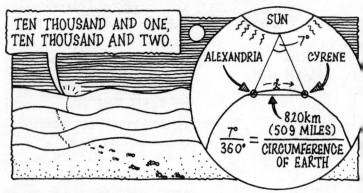

Smart eh? Sadly poor old Eratosthenes went blind in his old age and became so miserable he took his own life.

Archimedes (287-212 BC) was an all-round genius who invented pulleys and a method of raising water using a turning screw.

But his greatest achievement was to develop the principle of floating that states that the force of water supporting an object in the water is equal to the weight of the water it pushes aside.

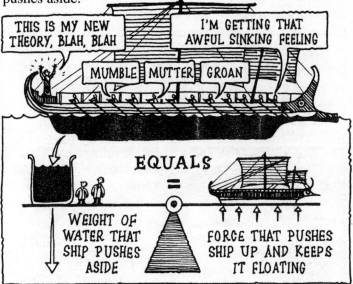

Whether he discovered this when he got in the bath is anyone's guess. Poor old Archimedes came a cropper in 212 BC when his city of Syracuse was captured by the Romans. Archimedes had a little misunderstanding with a Roman soldier but he got the point in the end. The point of the soldier's sword, that is.

Empedocles (490-430 BC) had lots of interests – in politics, medicine and predicting the future. (He charged people for this service.)

But his best known contribution to science was to claim that everything is made up of earth, air, fire or water, or a mixture of these things. This was a load of old rubbish although scientists believed in it for 2,000 years. But the best known fact about him was the way he died.

THE GREEK HERALD

430 BC

BARMY BOFFIN'S FIERY FATE

By our special reporter: OUCHMYTOES

Famous thinker Empedocles is dead. He perished inside volcano Mount Etna in Sicily. The barmy boffin jumped into the fiery crater in a crazed bid to become a god.

Empedocles, 60, had been acting oddly for some time, claiming to be the greatest thinker the world has ever known and declaring that he could become a god by leaping into the volcano.

A stunned follower paid tribute to the great man:

STUNNED FOLLOWER

"Old Empy was a mix of earth, air, fire and water but now he's mostly ashes. I'm afraid he didn't become a god so his reputation has gone up in smoke — but he was a lava-ly man."

BY-STANDERS REPORTED A BACON-LIKE PONG

And Empedocles wasn't the only ancient Greek scientist to meet a violent fate...

Deadly secrets

Syracuse, 405 BC

A great shout of horror rang through the palace. Guards dashed towards the hall and slave women cowered in the shadows. Outside, a teenage slave boy mopped his brow with a scrap of coarse linen.

"It was horrible. Horrible!" he cried.

"What's wrong Alexander?" said the old porter anxiously.

"It was horrible. I'm going to be sick!" gasped the youngster, propping himself against a pillar. His face was ghastly white and sweaty. The old man shook the boy's shoulder.

"What's horrible – what's happened in there?" he said urgently.

Alexander took a deep gulp of air.

"It was that Spartan woman – Tymicha. You remember King Dionysius captured her?"

The old man nodded. "She was one of that weirdo commune in Croton – wasn't she? Used to be run by that mathematician Pythagoras before the local people turned against them and slit their throats."

The young lad glared up at the old man. "I don't need reminding of that, Lysander, I've seen enough nasty sights today!" he said fiercely.

"So what happened in there?" asked Lysander, a puzzled frown creasing his lined forehead.

"The King ordered the woman to tell him all about the secret discoveries of the commune. About science – forces that make arrows fly and how the body works and all that."

"Yeah, he can be quite forceful, can young Dionysius."

"Well, no he was quite nice, actually. He even offered her a fortune."

"So she spilled the beans then? I know I would," the old man chuckled.

"No – she puffed herself up and bunched her fists and told everyone the secrets of science aren't for sale."

"So what are they, I wonder."

"I dunno," said the lad vaguely. "I heard two of the King's advisers saying they were supposed to be about numbers and how they control the universe. They said the woman knows about healing and setting broken bones so they mend and all that stuff. But anyway, the Spartan woman wouldn't tell."

The old man sadly shook his head.

"Oh dear – I expect that's when things turned nasty."

The boy shuddered.

"It certainly did. I mean you'd think that being a

scientist she'd have a bit of brains. You don't cross Dionysius – even I know that. The king was just listing the tortures available when..."

Well, what do you think happened next?
a) The scientist bit her toenails to show she wasn't afraid. This was a deadly insult to the king.
b) She cut off her little finger to prove how tough she was.
c) She bit off her own tongue to show she would never talk. She spat the grisly item at the king.

Answer: c) Members of the community were sworn to preserve the secrets of their discoveries even to the death.

A boring historian says...

This is probably just a legend. But a community of scientists did exist in Croton, in Italy, and it was destroyed by the local people. The group was set up by mathematician Pythagoras (582–500 BC) in 530 BC and they spent their time studying maths, developing scientific theories (since lost) and healing the sick. And they had strict rules about keeping their discoveries secret.

One scientist who didn't keep quiet about his ideas was a brainy doctor's son who became the teacher of a king. He was often wrong but for 1,800 years he was the most famous Greek scientist in the world.

And his name?

AMAZING ARISTOTLE

Imagine being famous. You could be on the telly and open supermarkets and stay in posh hotels and get people hanging around outside your house begging for an autograph.

If the scientist in this chapter was still alive today he would be as famous as that. And I don't mean famous for being 2,400 years old either. He would be famous for pioneering science and writing bestselling books describing his discoveries.

Here's his story.

Horrible Science Hall of Fame: Aristotle
(384-322 BC) Nationality: Greek

Aristotle's mum and dad died when he was young. Without parents to keep him in order he became a bit of a juvenile delinquent and blew his money on wild parties.

But when he was 17, Aristotle had a change of heart. He went to study in

Athens with philosopher Plato. Here the lessons were relaxed and easy-going and the pupils were encouraged to find things out for themselves. Don't you wish your school was like that?

Aristotle liked the school so much he became a teacher there and stayed 20 years. Eventually Plato died and his nephew took over the school. The nephew was heavily into maths which Aristotle hated (I don't blame him), so he went travelling in Turkey, advising local rulers on political matters and studying nature. Eventually, in 343 BC, he was invited to Macedon in Greece to teach the future ruler, Alexander the Great (356-323 BC).

Brilliant biology, futile physics and awful astronomy

Aristotle was interested in everything (except maths, of course). He wrote loads of books about nature and natural forces and in doing so he founded the sciences of biology and physics – so now you know who's to blame.

Aristotle was brilliant at biology. He wrote about 500 different types of creature and personally cut up 50 of them to see how they worked. And he realized that dolphins weren't fish because they fed their young on milk and didn't have gills. He was the first person to cut open a developing hen's egg and then describe how the ugly little unborn chick develops before it hatches. Could you do this – or would you chicken out?

But Aristotle was less good at physics and astronomy and although his ideas must have seemed quite sensible at the time, we now know that he got a lot of things wrong. And when I say wrong, I mean he sometimes got totally the wrong end of the stick. But his ideas were a big step forward, as they gave people sensible-sounding explanations for lots of things. For example, Aristotle said that...

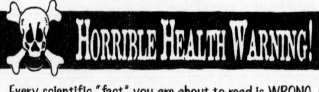

HORRIBLE HEALTH WARNING!

Every scientific "fact" you are about to read is WRONG. Not just mildly incorrect or even half-true. We're talking utter rubbish, drivel, clap-trap, humbug and poppycock. So copying this next bit for your science homework is about as clever as walking into a lion's den with a sign saying "HI, I'M LUNCH". We've asked a boring scientist to add a few corrections.

CHEEK!

BORING SCIENTIST

Physics by Aristotle

☞ A heavy object always falls faster than a lighter object. When an arrow falls to Earth it always drops down in a straight line.

> **WRONG** BOTH TIMES. (IF YOU DON'T BELIEVE ME TURN TO PAGES 75-6)

☞ Atoms don't exist.

> **WRONG** - EVERYTHING IS MADE UP OF ATOMS

☞ Everything is made up of earth, air, fire or water.

> **WRONG** - SCIENTISTS KNOW THAT EVERYTHING IS MADE UP OF A MIXTURE OF ATOMS - OBJECTS WHICH ARISTOTLE DIDN'T BELIEVE IN. BY THE WAY, IF ARISTOTLE'S THEORY SOUNDS FAMILIAR THAT'S BECAUSE IT IS. HE PINCHED IT FROM EMPEDOCLES!

Astronomy by Aristotle

☞ The moon is a perfectly smooth ball.

> **WRONG** - TRY LOOKING AT THE MOON WITH BINOCULARS AND YOU'LL SEE HE WAS WRONG. (OK, BINOCULARS WEREN'T INVENTED UNTIL THE 1890s SO YOU CAN'T BLAME ARISTOTLE FOR THIS.)

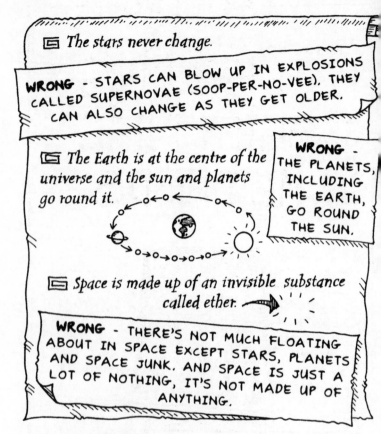

▣ The stars never change.

WRONG - STARS CAN BLOW UP IN EXPLOSIONS CALLED SUPERNOVAE (SOOP-PER-NO-VEE), THEY CAN ALSO CHANGE AS THEY GET OLDER.

▣ The Earth is at the centre of the universe and the sun and planets go round it.

WRONG - THE PLANETS, INCLUDING THE EARTH, GO ROUND THE SUN.

▣ Space is made up of an invisible substance called ether.

WRONG - THERE'S NOT MUCH FLOATING ABOUT IN SPACE EXCEPT STARS, PLANETS AND SPACE JUNK. AND SPACE IS JUST A LOT OF NOTHING, IT'S NOT MADE UP OF ANYTHING.

A nasty gut feeling

Aristotle died rather painfully of violent indigestion. This unhappy event proves that science can be a pain in the guts. But there's one thing even more painful if you're a scientist. More painful, even, than getting your answers wrong. And that's going about your job in the wrong way. This can cause some suffering scientific disasters.

Read on if you dare!

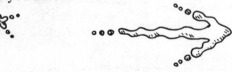

PART TWO

SUFFERING SCIENTIFIC METHODS

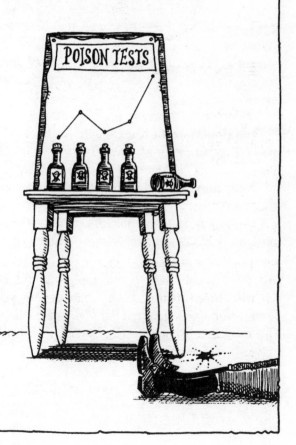

SCIENCE SYSTEMS SORTED

You know that scientists carefully test their ideas by experiments and observing things? Well, this kind of careful scientific approach didn't invent itself. People who were interested in science had to figure out that this was the best way to go about doing science. And it nearly didn't happen.

As you know, Aristotle was a great thinker – but you could say he was *too* famous, and that people took too much notice of what he said. Unfortunately for science, although Aristotle did a great job of observing dolphins or eggs he didn't think this was the best way to make scientific discoveries. Instead he believed that experts should argue out problems and the likes of you and me had to go along with what the experts said whether we liked it or not.

Yes, it's just like being back at school.

And if that wasn't bad enough, for the next 2,000 years powerful people and the Christian Church reckoned Aristotle was the greatest expert of the lot. So people believed him even when he was wrong. And that meant that even great thinkers believed that the best way to solve problems was to read books by experts like Aristotle and not observe things or carry out experiments for themselves.

Things only got better around 1600 as people began to make new discoveries and to find out that Aristotle was wrong. But the idea of taking a new look at the way in which people found out about the world came not from a scientist but from a lawyer. A brainy lawyer with a curious interest in frozen chickens.

And it was all thanks to...

Brainy Bacon and scientific science

Francis Bacon (1561-1626) wasn't a scientist – he was a lawyer. In fact, he was a pretty good lawyer who served two English monarchs, Elizabeth I (1533-1603) and James I (1566-1625).

In 1621 Francis was made Lord Chancellor – that's the top lawyer in the country – but five days later he was sacked for taking bribes. A bad thing for Bacon's career, but a GOOD thing for science.

Bacon now had the spare time to write a book arguing that knowledge about the world shouldn't depend on arguments and experts like Aristotle. Instead, said Bacon the lawyer...

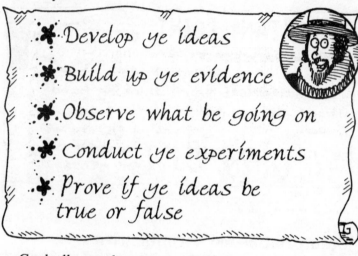

* Develop ye ideas
* Build up ye evidence
* Observe what be going on
* Conduct ye experiments
* Prove if ye ideas be true or false

Gradually people came to realize the value of working in this careful manner. And so, science as we know it was born. Of course, if you become a scientist that's what you'll be doing. But there's a problem – some experiments are *really* horrible.

Dare you try your hand at this lot...?

WHY NOT?

SUFFERING SCIENTIFIC EXPERIMENTS

Have you ever felt a little scared when you're doing a science experiment? Maybe there's a whiff in the air and it's not chemicals – it's danger. Perhaps you're handling poisonous substances or something that might blow up? Well cheer up, the story of science is full of experiments that left scientists suffering.

Look what happened to Robert Bunsen (1811-1899) and his pal Emil Fischer (1852-1919). Robert Bunsen was Professor of Chemistry at Heidelberg University in Germany. His achievements included discovering two new types of atom – caesium and rubidium. He also investigated really smelly chemicals such as those based on cacodyl (ca-co-dill). These made his clothes stink. Emil Fischer's wife said:

First I would like to wash Bunsen and then I would like to kiss him because he is such a charming man.

Teacher's tea-break teaser

Do you have Bunsen burners in your school? If so, after a science lesson you can ask your teacher:

DID ROBERT BUNSEN INVENT THIS BUNSEN BURNER?

Answer: The Bunsen burner was named after Bunsen, but he didn't invent it. It was probably developed by one of his assistants, Peter Desdega.

Now back to the story.

I expect Mrs Fischer was used to the effects of unpleasant chemicals on her husband. Emil Fischer was a jolly man who enjoyed playing the piano and eating good food. But one of the chemicals he discovered must have put everyone else off their supper. It caused a disgusting skin condition that made his skin peel off in strips. And then something happened that really spoilt his social life.

In the early 1880s he discovered skatole (scat-o-lee). This is one of the chemicals found in the guts that makes farts smelly. Later on that day a group of his students set off for their homes in another town. They tried to check in at a hotel for the night. But the smell of the skatole on their clothes was so revolting the hotelier thought they had a major bottom-burp problem. So they were turned away.

Really risky experiments
But at least they didn't suffer as much as the scientists who tried something really risky...

Frozen Francis
Remember Francis Bacon and how keen he was on experiments? In April 1626 he may have changed his mind. Well, he definitely would have done if he had lived long enough...

Ye olde Daily News

9 April 1626

CHICKEN KILLS BACON!

Ex-Lord Chancellor Francis Bacon is dead.

BERT

According to his driver, Bert, Bacon was in his coach admiring the snow when he decided on an experiment. "He wanted to see whether snow would preserve a dead chicken - I thought he was off his trolley."

THE KILLER CHICKEN

Bacon bought a dead chicken from a local peasant and was stuffing snow into its guts when he was taken ill. Said driver Bert, "Then he threw up and the smell was 'orrible. His

lordship looked almost as bad as the chicken." A doctor was called but he reported: "He's got a severe stomach chill that's spread to his lungs. I can't save Frank's bacon."

In the early days of science there was no such thing as safety equipment such as goggles and protective suits and proper face masks. And look what happened...

Terrible tests

1 Robert Bunsen went blind in one eye and nearly killed himself investigating poisonous arsenic.

SO TELL ME, MR BUNSEN, ARE YOU HAPPY IN YOUR WORK?

2 French chemist Pierre Dulong (1785-1838) hit lucky in 1811. He found a new chemical called nitrogen trichloride (ni-tro-jen try-klor-ride). Well, that wasn't so lucky because the powerful chemical dissolved Pierre's eyeball and two of his fingers.

3 Electricity can be shockingly dangerous. In 1745 Dutch scientist Pieter van Musschenbroek (1692-1761) filled a metal container with water and linked it to a device that made static electricity through a brass rod. The electrical charge built up in the water and when the scientist's assistant touched it by accident he got a nasty shock. Shortly afterwards German scientist Ewald von Kleist (1700-1748) suffered a similar accident and said:

I wouldn't take another shock to be the King of France.

Mind you, becoming the ruler of France would be a shock for most people.

4 German chemist Justus von Liebig (1803-1873) was well-liked by the students he taught at the University of Giessen. One day he asked for volunteers to test a new acid. The students were just like really keen kids with a popular science teacher (yes, there are such people). Every hand shot up. So Justus dripped some of the acid on the bare arms of the volunteers. In fact, it turned out to be far more powerful than he thought and some of the volunteers were badly burned.

5 English scientist Edgar Adrian (1889-1977) was an expert on nerves. And he enjoyed testing how well his nerves reacted by driving really fast and recklessly. Of course, any passengers in the car would have had their nerves tested too!

eaky labs

Most scientists need somewhere to perform their experiments – in other words a laboratory. Over the years labs have come in all shapes and sizes. Just compare these two...

SELLWELL'S
ESTATE AGENTS

FOR SALE
Private island complete with castle and laboratory.
Castle Uraniberg, Hven Island, Denmark.
Sellwell's are delighted to offer this unique property with its own island and village full of well-behaved peasants. We understand that the castle was built by scientist and astronomer Tycho Brahe (1546-1601) in 1575.
The property in brief. . .

- Island with 40 farms, a village and 60 ponds full of fish to eat.

- A windmill, paper mill and dam.

- Two kennels for guard dogs.

- Castle with private lab and 5.2 metre (17 feet) thick walls.

- Two observatories to look at the stars.

SALE PRICE A VERY REASONABLE
£9,999,999

Bet you never knew!

Tycho Brahe had a nasty temper. When he was 19 he got into a midnight sword fight with another Danish nobleman over ... the answer to a maths problem. Is your maths homework worth a fight? The noble sliced the end of Tycho's nose off – I bet that put his nose out of joint. For the rest of his life Tycho wore a false nose made out of copper and silver. But he went on quarrelling and in 1597 he had to leave Hven after falling out with the Danish Royal Family.

FOR SALE
The shed, Paris.

A historic property, scene of the discovery of a new type of atom – radium – in 1898 by scientists Marie Curie and her husband Pierre. The property in brief...

⌂ Basically – a lean-to structure with a compact floor space. That's it.

⌂ Well ventilated (lots of holes). This is very useful for getting rid of poisonous fumes from any experiments you might want to perform.

⌂ Nice and cool in the summer (and winter).

⌂ Would suit keen DIY'er!

Price: any reasonable offer accepted. Any offer will do – oh all right, you're welcome to it.

Bet you never knew!

The shed was the only space available for the cash-strapped Curies. Marie Curie (1867-1934) and Pierre Curie (1859-1906) spent four years in the shed heating poisonous chemicals in a bid to find radium. A visiting German scientist, Wilhelm Ostwald, said:

> It was a cross between a stable and a potato cellar ... I would have thought it a practical joke...

Scientists are still hard at work in their labs and they're still using careful methods of observation and experiment similar to those described by Bacon 300 years ago. If they are successful and make a great discovery they could win the Nobel Prize.

A boring scientist says...

The Nobel Prizes were set up in 1901 using money given by the Swedish inventor of dynamite Alfred Nobel (1833–1896). There are prizes for people who have done most for physics, chemistry, medicine, literature and world peace. You get a gold medal 6.5 cm (2.6 inches across) and £250,000 — can't be bad. One day I might win one too. . . (Sigh.)

Test your teacher
How old was the youngest scientist to win the Nobel Prize?
a) 11
b) 45
c) 25

Answer: c) Does your dad help you with your science homework? Well, here's a fact to tell your dad next time you're having problems with your physics. Sir William Bragg (1862-1942) certainly helped his lad Lawrence (1890-1971). Together they found out how to study atoms from the way the X-rays spread outwards after passing through a crystal. In 1915 father and son got to share the Nobel Prize and young Lawrence was just 25.

Are you still wondering whether to be a scientist? Well, if so you'll be itching to read the next chapter.

MODERN SUFFERING SCIENTISTS

The first thing you need to decide if you're going to be a scientist is what type of science you are going to do. Now, in the 2,300 years since Aristotle science has gone a long way. It's developed into many branches each with its own specially trained scientists.

IMPORTANT POINT

This was happening about 1800. By then scientific knowledge had become so complicated that no single person could know it all. So scientists chose to specialize in one or other branch of science. Anyway, here's a handy guide to help you spot the main types of scientist.

Spot the scientist

○ **Astronomers**
○ These ones study outer space and everything in
○ it. They are interested in questions such as
○ how big the universe is and what conditions are
○ like on other planets. Since most astronomers
○ haven't been into space they depend on looking
○ through telescopes and sending probes to study
○ the night sky. Actually,
○ though, astronomers don't
○ spend much time looking
○ through their telescopes.
○ Computers analyse the
○ images automatically and
○ produce pictures for the
○ astronomers to look at.

FASCINATING SPACE PROBE

BORING ALIEN SPACESHIP

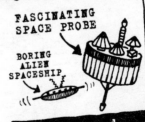

continued...

THIS ASTRONOMER HAS BEEN LOOKING THROUGH A TELESCOPE ALL NIGHT.

TIRED EYES FROM LACK OF SLEEP

MUG OF COFFEE TO KEEP AWAKE

Chemists

These concern themselves with chemicals and the various ways of mixing them together to make new substances. Because chemicals are made up of a particular arrangement of atoms, chemists are very interested in how the atoms join together and what pretty shapes they make when they're joined up.

TEST TUBE FOR MIXING CHEMICALS

GOGGLES TO PROTECT EYES FROM DANGEROUS CHEMICALS

RUBBER GLOVES

Biologists

These scientists investigate plants and animals and how they manage to survive without being eaten or dying of disease. Biologists also want to know the grisly details of how living things feed and grow and how they reproduce, that is to say, produce young (or seedlings, in the case of plants). Some biologists specialize in studying the human body and others look at cells - the tiny jelly-like objects that make up plants and animals.

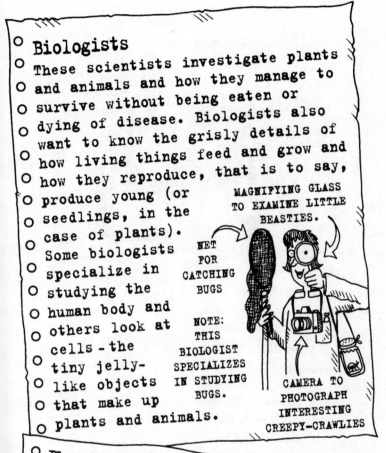

MAGNIFYING GLASS TO EXAMINE LITTLE BEASTIES.

NET FOR CATCHING BUGS

NOTE: THIS BIOLOGIST SPECIALIZES IN STUDYING BUGS.

CAMERA TO PHOTOGRAPH INTERESTING CREEPY-CRAWLIES

Physicists

They study energy and forces such as the force of gravity that makes pigeon droppings fall on your head. They look at how things move - that's whopping huge things like planets and stars and tiny things like atoms. Physicists are also

continued...

51

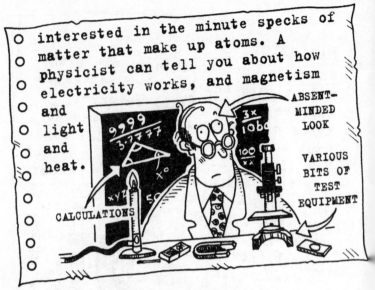

interested in the minute specks of matter that make up atoms. A physicist can tell you about how electricity works, and magnetism and light and heat.

CALCULATIONS

ABSENT-MINDED LOOK

VARIOUS BITS OF TEST EQUIPMENT

In this book you will come across all four types of scientist. Keep an eye open for them.

An out of this world project

Although these four types of scientist study different problems they sometimes come together to work on research which needs more than one type of expert. For example, a project on how creepy-crawlies behave in space might require...

• an astronomer to help plan the space route.

THEN THEY'LL "BEETLE" ALONG HERE FOR 3,000 MILES

• a physicist to build the rocket.

• a chemist to mix the rocket fuel.

• a biologist to study the bugs and look after them.

Obviously the bigger the project, the more scientists will be involved in it. Huge projects like those organized by the American NASA space programme employ hundreds of scientists. But whatever they're up to, the scientists have got one thing in common. They all use computers for their work. Let's take a closer look at that amazing creepy-crawlies-in-space project.

The astronomer uses the computer to calculate the orbit for the space lab containing the creepy-crawlies. A computer simulation will show where the main bits of space junk that you've got to avoid bashing into are. Meanwhile, the physicist is using a computer to calculate the stresses on the rockets, the effects of the cold temperature of space on the metal, the right amount of fuel to carry relative to the amount of weight that needs to be lifted off the ground and other fascinating topics – well, fascinating if you're a physicist.

The chemist has been busy using another computer simulation program to work out how the different chemicals in the fuel mixture will react when they are exploding at high temperatures. Will they power the rocket effectively? Or will they blow it up? And the biologist has no wish to go into space to look after the bugs. So she is working on a computer program to control the amount of light and food they are given automatically.

Then the rocket is ready to head for the stars with the creepy-crawlies safely on board. 10, 9, 8, 7...

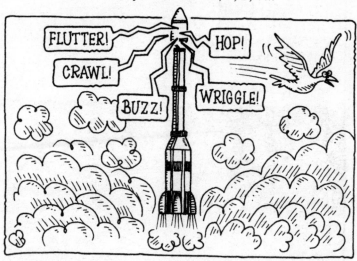

And that's where we've got to leave the story. You'll be pleased to know that the rocket blasts off safely and the bugs spend the next few weeks happily orbiting the Earth and the scientists spend the time happily monitoring the bugs. Oh well, talking about space, that's where we're going too: in the next chapter you can find out about the very first star-gazers.

And how they suffered.

PART THREE

SUFFERING
ASTRONOMERS

ANCIENT ASTRONOMERS

Our Stone Age family – the Ugs (remember them from page 12?) gazed at the skies in wonder like little kids today and tried to imagine where the stars came from and why they shine. And if that sounds boring, remember they didn't have telly in those far-off days.

Bet you never knew!
Some people think that Stonehenge and other rings of stone which were built in – surprise, surprise – the Stone Age are rather large clocks. They lined up with the rising of the sun at special times like Midsummer day and told the people who built them what day it was. Well, at least they didn't need batteries.

Meanwhile, in ancient India, Egypt, China and the Middle East, from about 3000 BC astronomers were staring at the night sky and giving themselves stiff necks. They were making measurements to find out where the stars are and how they appeared to move across the sky during a year in order to work out the details of the calendar.

Bet you never knew!
The native peoples of Central America also kept astronomical records. The Maya people, who were around from 2,600 BC to AD 900, calculated the orbit of Venus round the sun so accurately that they were only 14 seconds out.

Back in Europe, along came Aristotle and his dodgy theories. They were repeated by a writer called Ptolemy of Alexandria, who added that the sun and planets and stars were set in see-through balls made of crystal that moved around the Earth. All this was taken up by top people in the Church who thought it fitted in well with the stories in the Bible. So for the next 1,400 years there were no astronomical ideas in Europe because everyone thought that Aristotle had explained everything there was to know.

59

Bet you never knew!
One reason for this was that people felt that humans were the most important life-forms in the universe and Earth was the most important place in the universe and they couldn't imagine that it wouldn't be at the centre of the universe. Mind you, some people still think they're the centre of the universe.

GAG!

WELL MAYBE NOT THE MOST IMPORTANT— BUT I'VE GOT TO BE IN THE TOP TEN

Hunted Hypatia

Although everyone was happy to go along with Aristotle, astronomy was still being taught in schools and astronomers continued to plot the positions of the stars. And one ancient astronomer suffered a horrible fate. Hypatia of Alexandria (AD 375-415) wrote books on astronomy and mathematics. She also drew up tables showing the positions of the many stars in the night sky at different times of the year. And for this she designed an astrolabe (that's a device that measures the positions of stars). Unfortunately, the precise plans of Hypatia's astrolabe have been lost and Hypatia herself met a particularly sticky end.

Hypatia's sticky end

At the time, Alexandria was full of battles between supporters of rival religions: Jews, Christians and those who, like Hypatia, believed in the old Roman gods. The Christians didn't like Hypatia because she was a friend of their enemy, Orestes, the Roman who happened to be ruling Egypt. With me so far? When Orestes fell out with Cyril (376-444), the leading Christian in Alexandria, the Christians blamed Hypatia for the rift.

Hypatia's murder did its job. Orestes fled from Egypt and the murderers went unpunished.

So for the next 1,200 years there wasn't very much happening for astronomy in Europe. But elsewhere in the world there were some excellent astronomers. Like the person in the next chapter – he was a real star. Odd to think he started out as a *teacher*.

SCIENCE STAR OMAR

This chapter is about Ghiyath al-din Abu l'Fath Umar Ibn Ibrahim al-nisaburi al Khayyami. This is a bit of a mouthful and it must have taken ages for his mum to call him in for his tea.

Fortunately, he has gone down in history as...

Horrible Science Hall of Fame: Omar Khayyám
(AD 1048-1122) NATIONALITY: Persian

Omar was born in Khurasan in what is now Iran. Nothing is known about his family but the name Ibrahim means "tent maker" so maybe that's what his family did for a living. Young Omar must have had a good education because he became a teacher with an interest in scientific subjects. But he found it hard to study.

He later admitted that as a teacher he was so busy teaching he had little time to find out about the subject he

62

was supposed to be telling children about. Does your teacher have this problem – and dare you ask?

At least Omar managed to find time to write a book on algebra and another on music. Given a bit longer he might have written a book on musical maths! Later things started to look up.

A star is born

Around 1070 Omar made friends with an important judge Abu Tahir. The judge must have been into maths because Omar dedicated two more books on algebra to him...

Omar's work for the judge attracted the attention of the Sultan Jalal al-Din. And the Sultan gave Omar the job of looking after his astronomical observatory.

Omar was very happy and he spent the next 18 years tracking the movements of over 100 stars. And this is how he made his...

Crucial calendar

Seen from the Earth, the stars seem to move around us during the year. By 1079 Omar had enough information from his stargazing to calculate the exact length of a year.

... TAKE AWAY TWO AND DIVIDE BY FOUR AND... YES, **A YEAR IS 365·2424 DAYS!**

In fact, he was just 0.0002 days wrong. This meant that if you followed a calendar drawn up by Omar you'd find it was one day out in 5,000 years. Mind you, by then you might be too old to care too much even if you ended up missing your birthday or eating Christmas pudding on Boxing Day! (Our present calendar is actually less accurate than Omar's because it loses one day in 3,333 years.)

SO IF I LIVE TO BE 1,216,545 YEARS OLD, I'LL LOSE A WHOLE YEAR!

SIGH!

Omar advised the Sultan to re-jig the calendar to fit in with his newly calculated year. But then things began to go wrong.

First, the Sultan died.

Omar thought things could carry on because he was a pal of the Grand Vizier – the Persian Prime Minister.

But the Sultan's queen seized power. She quarrelled with the Vizier and he was murdered by a mysterious killer.

Any friend of the Vizier wasn't exactly flavour of the month with the queen. Omar's observatory was closed down.

Omar wrote a book claiming that the ancient rulers of Persia were really nice people. Kind-hearted and generous – especially to astronomers like Omar.

But the queen was definitely not amused by this unsubtle hint and not surprisingly Omar was never given another job.

Bet you never knew!
Omar was an excellent poet and he is better known in Europe for his verse, rather than for his study of the uni-verse, ha ha.

Futile fortune-telling

One of Omar's jobs was to draw up horoscopes based on the positions of the stars to foretell the future for important people. He wasted loads of time on this even though he secretly didn't believe in it. (Of course, people still believe in this practice, known as astrology, but you'd never catch a modern scientist peeping at their horoscope in the paper.)

Meanwhile, back in Europe, people still believed in Aristotle's dodgy theories about the universe. And it took another 400 years for an astronomer to come along who was clever enough to show that old Aristotle's theories were wrong.

CLEVER COPERNICUS

Nicolaus Copernicus was lucky. Dead lucky. You can say that because he was dead by the time his ideas finally appeared in print. But that was a good thing because it saved him from a grisly fate at the hands of the Church.

Horrible Science Hall of Fame: Nicolaus Copernicus (1473-1543) NATIONALITY: Polish

When Nicolaus was just ten years old his dad, a rich merchant, died and the young boy went to live with his uncle. In those days it was handy having an uncle who happened to be a rich, powerful bishop. As a result young Nick got loads of pocket money, and he was able to stay in education, studying for 15 years after he left school. (OK, I realize that this wouldn't be your idea of luck but young Nick was keen to learn.) After a spell at university in Poland studying maths, he made for Italy and studied medicine and law at three more universities.

IMPORTANT POINT

Italy was an exciting place at this time. Scholars were rediscovering ancient Greek and Roman writings that had mouldered in dusty old monasteries. And educated people were once more taking an interest in science and the ideas of the Greeks.

A mixed-up medicine

As a result of his medical studies Nick invented a new medicine. Here's the recipe...

Nick claimed that if you took this medicine twice a day it would cure anything. Well, possibly not stomach ache – it would *give* you stomach ache and cure nothing else.

I expect his uncle was wondering when Nick would stop studying and get himself a proper job. So whilst Nick was away his uncle arranged to have a job waiting for him at home – as a canon of Frauenburg Cathedral.

Canons did administration work but Nick had plenty of time for his hobby of astronomy. He'd got interested in astronomy at Bologna (one of the universities he'd studied at in Italy) after he saw an eclipse of the moon. Luckily his nice kind uncle built him a tower so he could get a good view of the stars.

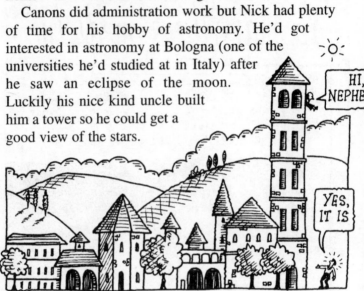

HI, NEPHE

YES, IT IS

What goes around...

Copernicus noticed that the stars seem to move away from or closer to the Earth in the course of the year. And he reasoned that the Earth must be moving in a big circle through space. So it followed that the Earth must be going round the sun, instead of the sun going round the Earth.

Nick didn't get it totally right. Like Ptolomy he thought the planets were fixed in crystal balls. Of course, if he had a real crystal ball he would have known that this theory was wrong. In 1543 Nick had a stroke (that's a kind of brain seizure). He couldn't move or talk but someone brought him a copy of his book explaining his theory with its ink still wet. He was holding it when he died.

Copernicus was quite lucky to die before the Church

bigwigs got to read his book. Supposing he'd lived longer, then he might eventually have died in a rather more painful way. Burnt alive at the stake because this was the penalty for heresy – ideas attacking the Church. Remember, the Church taught that Aristotle was right when he claimed the sun went round the Earth. But Nicholas Copernicus wasn't the only scientist to face this terrible death.

Bet you never knew!
Giodano Bruno (1548-1600) was an Italian monk who developed views that made his bosses in the Church chew the carpet. Bruno believed:

▶ COPERNICUS WAS RIGHT - THE EARTH GOES ROUND THE SUN

▶ THE EARTH IS ALIVE BECAUSE IT MOVES THROUGH SPACE

▶ THE UNIVERSE IS HUGE AND EVERYTHING IN IT IS MADE UP OF ATOMS.

Bruno didn't do much in the way of original research (he used reason and speculation) – but two of his ideas were right. Can you spot which ones?

Bruno v. the Inquisition

Bruno wandered round Europe teaching and writing for a living. Then he decided to return to Italy – it was a fatal mistake. Bruno had been offered a job teaching in Venice and he reckoned that his employer would protect him. He didn't. Instead, Bruno was arrested by the dreaded Inquisition. This was the organization within the Church charged with stamping out heresy, using torture and execution if necesary. After seven years in prison Bruno was tried as a heretic and there could be only one verdict.

An unhappy ending

Warning: If you don't like unhappy endings cover your eyes before reading this.

The good news:
The Chief Judge said:

HE WILL BE PUNISHED AS MERCIFULLY AS POSSIBLE, AND WITHOUT SHEDDING OF HIS BLOOD

THAT DOESN'T SOUND TOO BAD

The bad news:

The sentence was carried out immediately, on 8 February 1600. Poor old Bruno. He wanted a blaze of scientific glory but he didn't get quite the blaze he bargained for. But Bruno wasn't the only scientist who faced this terrible fate...

GALLANT GALILEO

In 1633, Galileo Galilei was famous as an astronomer and a great all-round scientist. But in that year he too faced torture and death at the hands of the Inquisition. Would Galileo go the same way as Bruno?

Horrible Science Hall of Fame: Galileo Galilei (1564-1642) NATIONALITY: Italian

Young Galileo was seriously into maths. In fact, he was so good at maths that he became Professor of Mathematics at Pisa University when he was only 25. Then he became interested in science after reading books by Bruno and Copernicus. The books convinced Galileo that the Earth went round the sun.

IMPORTANT POINT

Scientists have been interested in different kinds of science at different times in history. Thanks to Copernicus, in the century after 1550 astronomy was definitely the thing to study. And there were famous astronomers like Galileo who did just that.

Fantastic physics discoveries

Meanwhile Galileo was making huge discoveries that weren't to do with astronomy – but physics. For example, he proved, by carefully watching a pendulum, that each of its swings always took the same time no matter how big it was. And he explained this in terms of mathematical rules, the first time that anyone had ever used maths to describe how an object moves. Thanks to this discovery, Dutch scientist Christiaan Huygens (1629-1693) built the world's first pendulum clock – a clock that used the regular swing of the pendulum to keep time.

Dare you discover ... two more of Galileo's physics discoveries?

Experiment 1

All you need is...
A rubber ball
A table

All you do is...
Roll the ball along the table so it falls off the end.

What does the ball do when it gets to the edge of the table?
a) It drops straight down in a straight line.
b) It runs on through the air for a few centimetres before dropping down in a straight line.
c) It falls in a curved line.

HORRIBLE HEALTH WARNING!

Do not perform this experiment at meal times or when there are priceless ornaments on the table. Otherwise you will have to clear up the mess and eat your meals on the floor with the cat.

...AND YOU'RE NOT USING MY BOWL

PUSSY

Answer: c) Aristotle had said that when something falls down it suddenly drops downwards in a straight line, remember? But he never checked his idea with an experiment. Galileo's discovery helped gunners fire their cannon more accurately – so take cover!

Experiment 2

All you need is...
A table-tennis ball
A ball of plasticine or blutak of exactly the same size.

All you do is...
1 Drop both balls over the banister of your stairs or out of a first floor window.

Which ball hits the ground first?
a) The heavier plasticine or blutak ball.
b) The lighter table tennis ball.
c) They hit the ground at the same time.

HORRIBLE HEALTH WARNING!
You did remember to check there was no one underneath? Sorry, I should have warned you earlier.

Answer:
c) Aristotle said heavier objects fall quicker than lighter objects. By rolling balls of different weights and timing their speeds, Galileo proved Aristotle was wrong. As long as they are the same size and not affected by any other force, heavy and light objects accelerate (speed up) towards the ground together at the same rate. That's because gravity acts on them in the same way. Galileo didn't figure that bit out and didn't realize that gravity was at work. (This was left to Isaac Newton: see page 166.) But Galileo's work gave Newton his starting point.

So how did you get on? If you got both questions right you might be on your way to being a great scientist like Galileo. Oh well, hope you don't get arrested and threatened with torture and death. Because that's what happened to Galileo.

Star-struck Galileo

In 1609 Galileo switched from being a physicist to being an astronomer. He heard about the newly-invented telescope, built his own and used it to discover four moons of Jupiter and the mountains on the moon. These discoveries proved once again that Aristotle's theories were wrong – the moon wasn't a perfect round ball as the ancient Greeks believed, it had bumps and craters.

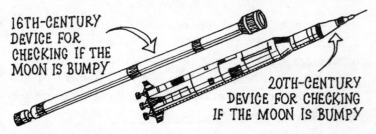

16TH-CENTURY DEVICE FOR CHECKING IF THE MOON IS BUMPY

20TH-CENTURY DEVICE FOR CHECKING IF THE MOON IS BUMPY

Most important of all Galileo watched as the planets Venus and Saturn travelled round the sun. So the Earth wasn't the centre of the solar system after all. Copernicus and Bruno were RIGHT! Galileo couldn't wait to tell everyone so he wrote a book in 1610 which made this case. It was a BIG mistake...

TO YE PUBLISHERS

A time of trial

Galileo was brilliant at nearly everything. A brilliant artist a brilliant writer, a brilliant musician and of course a brilliant scientist. The only thing he wasn't brilliant at was being modest.

As a result he made powerful enemies – especially in the Church. In 1633 after a series of warnings against his teaching, Galileo was put on trial before the Inquisition The charge was heresy, and the likely punishment – death by burning. Here's an exclusive peek at what Galileo's file might have looked like.

Of course, any fool knows the Sun goes round the Earth. If the Earth moved, the birds would fall off the trees wouldn't they?

ARGH!

BACKGROUND:

Galileo promised to give up his ideas in 1616. But last year he published a book again making fun of the Church's teaching and putting forward his wicked ideas. He says that all views are covered in the book which is based on a conversation between three people. But the character who backs our views is called Simplicius – er, we think that means we're supposed to be stupid. Well, now Galileo's really gone and done it.

THE BURNING QUESTION

Will Galileo admit he's wrong...? The first step is to show him the instruments of torture. Like the rack for stretching a person until their leg and arm bones plop out of their sockets. (It's known in the trade as "a long stretch in prison".) Then the red hot pincers, and the rope that goes round the head with tightening knots that make the eyeballs fall out. Then we really turn up the heat – at the stake.

What happened next?
A boring historian says...

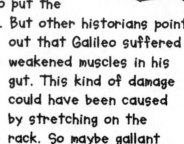

We historians aren't too sure. Some say that Galileo was too famous to be tortured. The Inquisition just showed him the torture chamber to put the frighteners on him. But other historians point out that Galileo suffered weakened muscles in his gut. This kind of damage could have been caused by stretching on the rack. So maybe gallant Galileo ended up just a bit taller.

BEFORE

AFTER

But Galileo didn't die. To save his life he confessed that the Earth didn't go round the sun. He said:

I curse and detest the aforesaid errors and heresies and I swear that I will never more ... say ... anything that will give rise to a similar suspicion of me.

And according to legend he muttered under his breath:

But the Earth still moves.

Galileo was sentenced to life imprisonment. He was locked up in his own home and never released. Eventually he went blind and had to give up scientific work because he had no one to help him.

Bet you never knew!

Galileo and Bruno weren't the only astronomers in trouble. Johann Kepler (1571-1630) was a German astronomer who used maths to show how the planets move round the sun in flattened circles known as ellipses (ee-lip-sees). But he fancied himself as a science fiction author. In 1610 he wrote a story in which his mum was a witch who made contact with alien monsters from the moon. Somebody showed the story to the authorities, and they thought it was true! The harmless old woman was dragged from her house and threatened with torture for being a witch! Kepler got his mum released by writing letters to important people.

THANKS SON. NOW, WHY WAS I ARRESTED?

ER, SOMEONE WAS TELLING STORIES ABOUT YOU

Thanks to the work of Galileo and Kepler, astronomers all over Europe were using their telescopes to gaze at the skies and plot the positions of the stars and planets. Everywhere except inside the Church people accepted that the Earth really does go round the sun. But there was much more to discover as German-born English astronomer William Herschel found out. But he was lucky – he had the best sister in the world to help him.

Read on and find out why...

A BROTHER WHO LIKES HIS SISTER . . . I'VE GOTTA READ THIS!

A LONG-SUFFERING SISTER

In 1782 William Herschel became Britain's top astronomer – the Astronomer Royal. He had just discovered the planet Uranus and over the next few years he found many new stars and comets. In 1783 he found a new type of light wave called infrared.

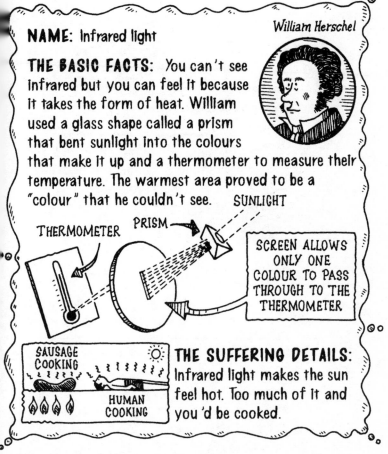

NAME: Infrared light

William Herschel

THE BASIC FACTS: You can't see infrared but you can feel it because it takes the form of heat. William used a glass shape called a prism that bent sunlight into the colours that make it up and a thermometer to measure their temperature. The warmest area proved to be a "colour" that he couldn't see.

SUNLIGHT

THERMOMETER

PRISM

SCREEN ALLOWS ONLY ONE COLOUR TO PASS THROUGH TO THE THERMOMETER

SAUSAGE COOKING

HUMAN COOKING

THE SUFFERING DETAILS: Infrared light makes the sun feel hot. Too much of it and you'd be cooked.

What is less well known is that William owed much of his success to a remarkable woman: his sister, Caroline.

Horrible Science Hall of Fame: Caroline Herschel
(1750-1848) NATIONALITY: German/ British

When Caroline was a little girl her dad told her:

And her mum added:

So young Caroline was given next to no education. Whilst her brothers learnt music from their musician dad, Caroline's mum forced her to learn how to cook and clean and mend her brother's smelly old clothes.

84

If Caroline kept a secret diary it might have looked like this.

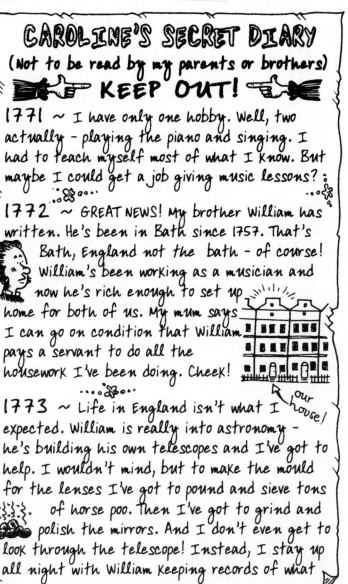

CAROLINE'S SECRET DIARY
(Not to be read by my parents or brothers)
KEEP OUT!

1771 ~ I have only one hobby. Well, two actually – playing the piano and singing. I had to teach myself most of what I know. But maybe I could get a job giving music lessons?

1772 ~ GREAT NEWS! My brother William has written. He's been in Bath since 1757. That's Bath, England not the bath – of course! William's been working as a musician and now he's rich enough to set up home for both of us. My mum says I can go on condition that William pays a servant to do all the housework I've been doing. Cheek!

our house!

1773 ~ Life in England isn't what I expected. William is really into astronomy – he's building his own telescopes and I've got to help. I wouldn't mind, but to make the mould for the lenses I've got to pound and sieve tons of horse poo. Then I've got to grind and polish the mirrors. And I don't even get to look through the telescope! Instead, I stay up all night with William keeping records of what he sees and feeding him using a long spoon because he's too busy to eat properly. And during the day I do all the housework just like I did in Germany. What a life!

1783 ~ Last Christmas William was back in Germany visiting the relatives. So I had a sly peep at the stars through one of his telescopes and found a previously unknown nebula - that's a giant cloud of distant stars in space. WOW!

1786 ~ My nice kind brother has made me my very own telescope (well, I helped with the horse-poo pounding) and I've already discovered a new comet!

WOW!

Caroline's comets

Caroline went on to discover seven more comets and to list all the main stars. This became a vital source of information for astronomers but Caroline was the kind of person who was less big-headed than a tiny little squeaking mouse. She once said:

I did nothing for my brother but what a well-trained puppy dog would have done.

Rubbish. Well-trained puppy dogs fetch their leads and yelp to go out for walkies. And if they're not quite so well trained they chew your slippers and pee behind the sofa. Caroline catalogued hundreds of stars and wrote reports and proved to be a great astronomer in her own right.

Thanks – but no thanks?

It took a long time for other astronomers to realize the value of Caroline's work. But they did in the end and in her old age she was awarded medals by the Royal Astronomical Society and the King of Prussia.

But life wasn't totally happy. In 1788 William married and poor Caroline had to move out of the house they shared. History doesn't record whether William ever bothered to say "Ta very much" for Caroline's years of devoted assistance.

Meanwhile astronomers continued to make dramatic discoveries. Tremendous breakthroughs that have changed our entire view of the universe. Read on – and discover:

MODERN STAR-GAZERS

In 1929 US astronomer Edwin Hubble (1889-1953) turned the universe upside down. Well, OK, not literally, but he certainly changed the way scientists see the universe. He noticed that no matter in what direction you look, the galaxies – the vast clusters of stars that make up the universe – are speeding away from us.

Of course, that could mean that the aliens just don't like us, but Hubble correctly reasoned that the universe was getting bigger just like a balloon when you blow it up. And if the universe is getting bigger then it stands to reason that it was once tiny. Hubble said that the universe started with an expansion (known as the Big Bang) and has been growing ever since. He became famous and mixed with film stars and some people say he got rather big-headed – so maybe his head was expanding too?

Teacher's tea-time teaser
All you need is an empty crisp packet and the kind of courage that is often mistaken for foolhardiness. Simply creep up behind a teacher at break and burst the crisp packet. When the teacher recovers, smile sweetly and enquire.

Answer: With luck the teacher will say "yes" rather crossly. In which case you can reply, "Ah, but I'm not sure that's right because sound is a wave of wobbling atoms in the air. And surely there isn't any air in space." This is true. The Big Bang wasn't a bang at all – it wasn't even a muffled squeak.

HORRIBLE HEALTH WARNING!

If you actually do this teaser, don't blame me – you're on your own, OK?

Tremendous telescopes

Since Hubble's day telescopes have got even more powerful. Today the biggest telescopes in the world are the Keck Telescopes at Mauna Kea, Hawaii. Each telescope picks up light from giant mirrors 10 metres (33 feet) across. And there is even a telescope in space; the Hubble space telescope was launched in 1990 – and no prizes for guessing who that's named after. And what's more, in the 1930s astronomers got a new kind of telescope.

In 1932 US radio engineer Karl Jansky (1905-1950) found that radio signals were

I'VE FOUND A HUGE GALAXY!

CAN I HAVE A BIT?

THE HUBBLE TELESCOPE SEARCHES DEEP INTO SPACE

coming from the stars and disrupting his radio equipment. (No, this wasn't the alien pop charts – they were radio waves that are given out naturally by stars just as stars also make light.) Soon scientists were building powerful radio receivers that could tune into these radio waves. In 1967 a radio telescope enabled science student Jocleyn Bell to detect the first known pulsar, a type of star that gives out huge amounts of radio waves.

THIS IS BELL RINGING FROM THE RADIO TELESCOPE, PROFESSOR. I'VE DISCOVERED A PULSAR!

Probes and planets

Ever since the 1960s scientists have been sending out space probes to photograph other planets – for example, probes actually landed on Mars in 1976 and again in 1998. And in 1969 humans first walked on the surface of the moon.

URGENT MESSAGE TO MISSION CONTROL... IT IS NOT MADE OF CHEESE... I REPEAT, THE MOON IS NOT MADE OF CHEESE

Today scientists know far more about our neighbouring planets, and in the 1990s they even began to find other planets circling distant stars, just like the planets in the solar system circle the sun. Galileo would have been gob-smacked. But that's not all.

In the 1970s astronomers discovered black holes. These are stars that have burnt out and then collapsed in on themselves under the power of their own gravity. This gravity is so strong that even light can't escape from them. Although the astronomers couldn't actually see the black holes they could detect X-rays given out by gas as it's sucked into the hole.

A black hole is like a giant plughole in space.

Its gravity is strong enough to do terrible things to anything that gets sucked into it.

Gravity is so strong that the difference between the force acting on the rocket's front end and back end stretches it and pulls it apart.

Some of the most interesting work on black holes was done by British scientist Stephen Hawking. For example, in 1971 he used maths to calculate that there must have been tiny black holes in the early stages of the Big Bang. And in 1974 he found, again using maths, that black holes can lose heat. By then he was really warming to his subject, ha ha.

Bet you never knew!
Hawking is disabled by a muscle-wasting disease and can't move from his wheelchair. After another illness, surgeons had to cut out his voice box and now he can't talk. Instead, he types words into a computer and these are either displayed on a screen or spoken by a machine called a synthesiser which turns the computer code into sounds. Despite this, Hawking is world famous, the author of bestselling books, and has even starred in a pop video and an episode of Star Trek.

So how about you? Would you like to be a scientist working on astronomical research like Hubble or Hawking? Or maybe not? Well, whilst you're deliberating, why not read the next chapter? It's about a totally different science and a whole new gang of suffering scientists.

PART FOUR

SUFFERING CHEMISTS

AWFUL ALCHEMISTS

The Ug family were as thrilled by the various substances they saw around them as toddlers in a sandpit. Stuff like different coloured earth and rock that they could use to make colours for cave painting. This was the hottest new discovery in those days. Mrs Ug even ordered a catalogue...

PAINTS TO BRIGHTEN UP YOUR CAVE!!

MADE USING THE LATEST STONE AGE TECHNOLOGY!

LOVELY SOOTY BLACK COLOURS MADE FROM BURNT BONES.

TASTEFUL RUSTY RED MADE FROM MANGANESE OXIDE. A KIND OF METAL COMPOUND FOUND IN ROCKS.

PLUS NEW UNIQUE FORMULA MIX: FAT FROM DEAD ANIMALS AND REAL HUMAN PEE.

IT GOES ON A TREAT! GUARANTEED TO LAST FOR THOUSANDS OF YEARS!

These colours were found by trial and error but you might think that it would be easy for early people to learn how to investigate chemicals in a more scientific way. But you'd be wrong. Wrong because chemistry hadn't been invented yet (even Aristotle hadn't worked on chemistry). Instead, there was a peculiar and mysterious "science".

94

The dawn of alchemy

Alchemists aimed to turn cheap grotty metals such as boring old lead into glinting, glittering, glamorous gold. Yes, these people weren't so much spurred by scientific curiosity as plain good old-fashioned greed.

A boring historian says...

> There were alchemists in ancient Greece, India and China. We historians think the Chinese invented alchemy separately because their aim was a bit different — they were trying to find a special kind of gold that you could drink and would make you live for ever. Alchemy may have been spread between Greece and India by traders, although no one knows where it began.

A waste of time?

Alchemists spent much of their time heating and mixing metals in search of the magical combination that would make gold. In fact, in those days your alchemy teacher would be more likely to jabber magic spells than teach you experiments. Sounds more fun? But was it all a waste of time? Yes, and MUCH more of a waste of time than science lessons today.

TONGUE OF TOAD WITH CHEESY MOULD TURN THIS MIXTURE INTO GOLD!

ALCHEMIST

SCIENCE TEACHER

TWITTER, MOAN, STUTTER. WITTER, DRONE, MUTTER.

A boring scientist says...

Nowadays scientists know that everything is made of atoms and gold atoms are different in weight and in the number of electrons (see page 23) they have than, say, lead atoms. And there was no way that alchemists could change atoms using the technology they had.

Alchemy: the good news

Although the main aim of alchemy is as pointless as a bike with no wheels, the alchemists made loads of interesting discoveries. For example, Arab alchemist Jabir (721-815) found out how to boil vinegar to make a strong acid called acetic acid, but his greatest discovery was how to make another chemical, ammonia, by boiling urine – that's the posh word for pee. Alchemists also knew how to dry chemicals until they formed crystals. And they knew about distillation.

Suffering expressions

HOW'S YOUR DISTILLATION?

This still Asian what?

Answer: Dis-till-a-tion is a technique used in chemistry to separate out the chemicals in a liquid. All you do is heat the liquid till it boils and draw off the gas that comes off it into a container where it cools back into a liquid. Since different chemicals turn to gas at different temperatures, different chemicals will boil off one by one as the mixture heats up. So some will pass into the container and some will be left at the bottom of the boiling container as a revolting sludge.

And alchemists such as Maria the Jewess who lived in Alexandria in the 1st century AD invented equipment used by later scientists. Maria designed a boiler that could heat chemicals nice and slowly and a vessel for distilling chemicals.

But alchemy had a down side.

Alchemy: the bad news

Because alchemists were basically barking up the wrong tree, some were tempted to cheat. These people were *crooks*...

The Case Notes of Chief Inspector Gold

For 15 years I have pursued a ruthless and secretive gang of villains known as "the Alchemists". In this notebook I outline some of the techniques used by this villainous crew.

One of the most shocking villains I encountered was the Empress Barbara.

CONTINUED →

Name: Barbara
Status: Former Empress of the Holy Roman Empire.

It appears that the Empress became "strapped for cash" following the sudden death of her husband, Sigismund, in 1437 and turned to alchemy to make money – she must have thought it was a golden opportunity. My informant, John of Laaz, visited the lady and she showed him how to make fake gold and silver.

The gold is made by mixing iron with the yellow herb saffron for its colour, together with a type of copper and other chemicals. The fake silver includes poisons such as mercury and arsenic.

> I saw nothing but lying and deception and I reproached her. She was going to have me thrown into prison but with God's help I managed to get away.

Clearly this woman is a menace to society, and the public should be on their guard against fake silver and gold at all times. Remember _nothing_ is as good as gold.

FAKE GOLD FAKE SILVER

CROWN SAFFRON ARSENIC MERCURY

It took scientists years and years to prove that alchemy didn't work. But meanwhile in 1661, inspired by the writings of Bacon, a sickly Irish-born chemist named Robert Boyle (1627-1691) wrote a book suggesting (although he couldn't yet prove) a new theory about chemicals.

Suffering scientists fact file

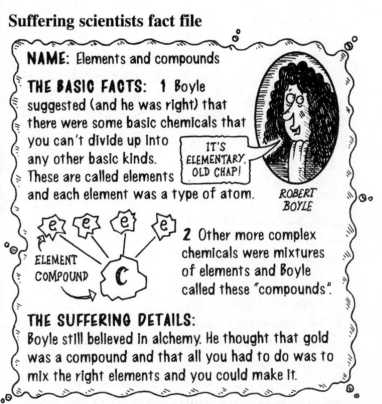

NAME: Elements and compounds

THE BASIC FACTS: 1 Boyle suggested (and he was right) that there were some basic chemicals that you can't divide up into any other basic kinds. These are called elements and each element was a type of atom.

IT'S ELEMENTARY, OLD CHAP!

ROBERT BOYLE

ELEMENT COMPOUND

2 Other more complex chemicals were mixtures of elements and Boyle called these "compounds".

THE SUFFERING DETAILS:
Boyle still believed in alchemy. He thought that gold was a compound and that all you had to do was to mix the right elements and you could make it.

At least Boyle encouraged scientists to mix chemicals in a more scientific way. And by doing so he founded a brand new science – chemistry. Bet you never knew that one of the greatest early chemists spent 60 years hiding from the world?

But you can find him in the next chapter.

CRANKY CAVENDISH

Let's imagine you're wandering around London in 1760. If you're lucky you might catch sight of a brilliant but shy scientist who made a hermit look like a party animal. Can you spot him?

No, he's gone.
So why was he so secretive?

Horrible Science Hall of Fame: Henry Cavendish
(1731-1810) NATIONALITY: British

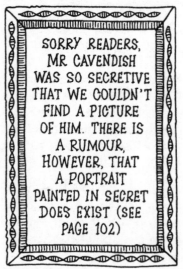

SORRY READERS, MR CAVENDISH WAS SO SECRETIVE THAT WE COULDN'T FIND A PICTURE OF HIM. THERE IS A RUMOUR, HOWEVER, THAT A PORTRAIT PAINTED IN SECRET DOES EXIST (SEE PAGE 102)

Henry Cavendish was rich. Very, very rich. In today's money he'd be worth well over £100,000,000 (That's one hundred million pounds). He was the son of a Lord, and the grandson of the Duke of Devonshire on his dad's side and the Duke of Kent on his mum's side. So right from the start young Henry went to a posh school and got loads of pocket money.

But money doesn't bring happiness. When he was two, Henry's mum died and the young boy became more and more shy and lonely. He went to university at Cambridge but left without taking a degree. He wasn't stupid – he had already shown an interest in science. No – he was scared of having to speak in public. (In those days to get a degree you had to answer questions in front of an audience of professors.)

He spent most of the rest of his life doing science experiments at home and avoiding talking to anyone. Of course, he never gave press interviews – but you know those glossy celebrity magazines that show pictures of smiling VIPs? Well, just imagine if they tried to feature Henry Cavendish.

MEGASTAR MAGAZINE

HENRY CAVENDISH
THE GOLDEN SCIENTIST

~ by Randel Scandel ~

This week *Megastar* gets an exclusive glimpse inside the London home of Henry Cavendish, the legendary reclusive multi-millionaire who has dedicated his life to science.

It's taken two years to see him and he only agreed because he thought we were a science journal about the stars in the sky. Science is the only subject he ever talks about and then only to a few scientific friends. Despite his wealth, Mr Cavendish lives a simple life and hardly ever spends money.

He doesn't like talking to his servants and generally leaves notes saying what he wants for dinner. The servants revealed exclusively to *Megastar* that Mr Cavendish once caught sight of a maid. He was so upset at seeing another human that he sacked the girl on the spot. He then built a private staircase in his house so he could go up and down without being seen.

SACKED SERVANT

Mr Cavendish gave us a guided tour of his private lab in Clapham and told us some facts about science that we didn't understand. He speaks in a high shrill voice and he gets worried if anyone looks at him. In fact, whenever he goes into a room he squeaks loudly as a signal for everyone else to leave. This portrait had to be painted in secret.

It shows Henry in his favourite suit of violet velvet - he never wears anything else, apparently. But luckily the greasy food and chemical stains aren't too visible.

More odd scientists

Do you know any eccentric scientists? What about your science teacher. Do they have any peculiar habits? Perhaps they crack their knuckles or take rides on equipment trolleys or walk into lamp posts when they are wrapped up in thought.

Perhaps they fit in with the popular image of a mad scientist? If you decide to be a scientist would you want to be like this?

Here are some handy hints...

Lesson 1
Cycle down a school corridor.

Important note:
If you do this and get expelled it's not our fault – OK?

British scientist Edgar Adrian (1889-1977 – yes, the guy who enjoyed reckless driving) did this at his Cambridge lab. But he also discovered that nerve signals grow stronger the more the nerve is excited and won the Nobel Prize in 1932. So he got away with being a little odd.

Lesson 2
Eat horrible things in the interests of science.

Yes, I know you already eat school dinners but this is worse. Someone once showed British geologist (that's a scientist who studies rocks) William Buckland (1784-1856) the mummified heart of French King Louis XV1. But Buckland, who is famous for discovering that rocks can be built up in layers over time, was hungry. He shouted, "I have never feasted on the heart of a king before!" and started chewing on the grisly relic.

Lesson 3
Wear strange clothes to school.

SNIGGER! CHORTLE!

Scottish scientist William Murdock (1754-1839), who found out how to make gas from coal, went to job interviews wearing a home-made wooden top hat. Biologist Herbert Spencer (1820-1903) wore a one-piece outfit that looked like a baby suit. Of course, if teachers don't realize that you're a genius you could be sent home with a rude note for your parents.

Now back to Cavendish. So what was he up to in that secret laboratory of his?

Cavendish's secret notebooks
Imagine reporter Randel Scandel had managed to borrow Cavendish's secret lab notes. Here's what they might have looked like:

The Lab Notebook of ~Henry Cavendish~

NOT TO BE OPENED BY SERVANTS OR ANYONE ELSE.

KEEP OUT!

Working alone I have discovered a whole range of new gases. In 1766 I added acid to marble. A gas was given off that I call "fixed air".

Then I decided to drip some more acid on to iron. This time another gas was given off. It seemed lighter than air and burnt easily so I called it "fire air". I think there may be fire air in the air all around us.

A boring scientist says...
That's the gas now called carbon dioxide. It's used to put the bubbles in fizzy drinks and in some fire extinguishers.

← iron

A boring scientist says...
Sorry to interrupt again. This gas is now called hydrogen. It is indeed found in the air and in stars such as the sun. It's added to the margarine you spread on your toast to make the oils it contains more solid, like butter. And it's used to make exploding rocket fuel to send rockets to the moon.

I784 ~ I've had an idea for a new "fire air" experiment.

First I get a pig's bladder. (Yuck - I had to leave a note to get one of the servants to wash it for me. Well, I wasn't going to actually TALK to them, was I?)

Next, I put it in a strong glass container and fill the bladder with two parts "fire air" and one part oxygen. (Oxygen is another gas that is in the air.) Now I put a candle flame to the opening of the bladder and TAKE COVER. . .

Oh no - footsteps, someone is coming!

BOOM!

Oh well, it was only a maid and the blast has scared her away! The flame made the fire gas explode. The bladder is in pieces and the inside of the glass container is misted up. What is this dampness? Is it pee? I thought I had the bladder washed! Oh well, better taste it and find out - slurp, lick. . . It's water! This proves that water is made up of two parts "fire air" and one part oxygen.

A boring scientist says. . . It's only me! Just to say, Cavendish was right again. Water is indeed made up of hydrogen and oxygen atoms.

Dare you discover ... how to make carbon dioxide?

You will need...
Half a glass of pure orange juice.
A level teaspoonful of baking soda.

All you do is...
Add the baking soda to the juice and stir well.

What happens?
a) The juice turns green.
b) The juice starts to bubble.
c) The juice feels warm to the touch.

Answer: b) The bubbles are caused by a chemical reaction between the acid in the juice and the baking soda. You can add some water, sugar and ice to the juice and enjoy your own home-made fizzy drink! Who said that science is always horrible?

Cavendish was so shy he never told anyone about most of his discoveries. They were brought to light 100 years later when another scientist, James Clerk Maxwell (1831-1879), came across Cavendish's notebooks. By then other scientists had made the same discoveries and grabbed the glory. Actually this was also the fate of the scientist in the next chapter. But unlike Cavendish he missed out on the glory not because he was shy but through bad luck. He was the unluckiest suffering scientist ever!

So grab yourself a box of hankies and read on...

SUFFERING SCHEELE

There is no doubt that Karl Scheele (1742-1786) was one of the world's greatest chemists. The problem was that people didn't appreciate him until long after he was dead. Which wasn't much good for suffering Scheele. Here's his story...

Horrible Science Hall of Fame: Karl Scheele (1742-1786) NATIONALITY: Swedish

Unlike many scientists in this book, Karl Scheele wasn't a university professor with a nice comfortable job. For most of his life he was a humble druggist's assistant. That meant he had to spend all day mixing chemicals for medicines. In his few spare hours he worked on his only hobby, chemistry.

Brilliant breakthroughs

Scheele managed to make a brilliant series of discoveries in the 1770s and 1780s. This was an incredible achievement because he had to work in cold miserable smelly rooms at strange hours of the night. Yet he discovered five elements (different types of atom, remember?).

Scheele's discoveries and their modern uses

Just to make this section more interesting we've added a fake element to the list of Scheele's discoveries. Can you spot it?

(TRYING TO SMELL IT UNDER WATER WILL KILL YOU AND NOT THE GERMS)

1 CHLORINE Use = Gives swimming pools that smell that gets up your nose. The chemical is actually added to kill germs and it's also added to your drinking water for this reason.

2 BARIUM Use = A metal that shows up on x-rays. Patients have to eat a vile-tasting chemical containing barium which then shows up blockages of their guts on x-rays.

3 MYMBLERINE Use = A powerful germ-killing substance often used to unblock particularly smelly sewers.

ARGH! MY KNEES, MAN! THIS CAR NEEDS MORE MANGANESE!

4 MANGANESE Use = Added to steel or aluminium metals to make them stronger. There might be some in your family's car.

109

5 MOLYBDENUM Use = Found in some lubricants - that's the posh word for the oil stuff that you put on your bike chain to stop it squeaking.

"OIL" BE NEEDIN' SOME FOR MY BIKE

6 NITROGEN Use = very cold nitrogen is used to preserve dead bodies. Some people pay to have their bodies preserved in this way in the hope that it might be possible to bring them back to life in the future. It's also an ingredient in some explosives and dyes.

HIS CHEQUE BOUNCED - SWITCH HIM OFF NURSE!

Answer: 3

More discoveries

He also discovered Scheele's green – a type of green dye based partly on copper and poisonous arsenic. And he found out how to extract phosphorus – an element useful in fertilizers – from animal bones. Previously it had only been found in human pee.

STOP THAT AND TRY SOME OF SCHEELE'S NEW FERTILIZER.

But Scheele's greatest discovery brought him no glory. Here's how it might have been reported.

The Köping Courier

21st September 1775

I WAS ROBBED!

Local scientist Karl Scheele is accusing two famous scientists of pinching his discovery.

Karl Scheele

"Four years ago," says Karl, 33, "I was heating a chemical called mercuric oxide when I found a new gas. I called it 'fire air' because things burnt in it." Karl claims he described the gas in a book - but it hasn't been published. "And now," moans Karl, "that cheeky Englishman Joseph Priestly and Frenchman Antoine Lavoisier are boasting they found the gas and they're calling it oxygen. And to think I even wrote to Lavoisier about my discovery! I've got to

Joseph Priestly   *Antoine Lavoisier*

stop them gassing about my gas! I'm gutted - I can tell you."

A boring historian says...

Scheele's book wasn't published until 1777 because famous Swedish scientist Tobern Bergman (1735-1784) never got round to writing the introduction.

111

A boring scientist adds...

Today oxygen is used in hospitals to help people with lung problems breathe, and divers and astronauts would soon die without their oxygen gas canisters. Oxygen is also used in welding where it is mixed with a burning gas called acetylene (a-set-aleen) to make a hot flame.

"WELD" DONE PIECE OF TOAST

TWO GASES MIX HERE

IMPORTANT POINT

To become a famous scientist it isn't enough to discover a new scientific law. You need a BIG mouth to tell the world about your discovery before someone else pops up and grabs the credit.

Dead disappointed

Worse still, Scheele had a really bad habit. He insisted on tasting and sniffing all the chemicals he discovered. This was actually a common habit of early chemists.

☠ HORRIBLE HEALTH WARNING!

Dangerous chemicals are not to be sniffed at – or tasted. This is an extremely unhealthy thing to do in your science class or at home. If you do this in order to copy Karl Scheele – you may well end up just like him. Dead. Scheele discovered several poisonous chemicals such as hydrogen cyanide. But they probably combined with overwork to cause his early death. He was just 43 years old.

More unlucky chemists

Mind you, Scheele wasn't the only unlucky chemist.

1 In 1848 German scientist Robert von Mayer (1814-1878) put forward the idea that when chemicals are mixed to form a new substance the chemicals involved don't gain or lose energy. The idea was correct but it was slow to catch on. Mayer got depressed and spent years in lunatic asylums.

2 In 1858 Scottish chemist Archibald Couper (1831-1892) was studying in Paris when he worked out the arrangement of atoms in a chemical called benzene (ben-zene). (This useful substance was later used in industrial dyes.)

But before the discovery could be announced German chemist Friedrich Kekulé (1829-1896) made the same discovery and got the credit. Couper eventually went mad with grief – so he went in-Seine in Paris!

3 In 1783 talented French chemist Nicolas Leblanc (1742-1806) won a competition set up by the French Academy of Sciences to make soda from salt. Soda was vital for soap-making and Leblanc looked set to clean up.

> GET RID OF NASTY BODY ODOUR WITH LEBLANC'S SOAP
>
> WASHES WHITER THAN WHITE!
>
> MADE BY HIS NEWLY INVENTED PROCESS USING SULPHURIC ACID.
>
> Before   After
>
> CHEAP SOAP & SIMPLE INGREDIENTS!

But the stingy Academy never paid the prize money and by 1806 Leblanc was very poor. Full of despair, he took his own life.

The scientists in this chapter were born losers. They'd have lost their heads if they hadn't been screwed on. Mind you, in the next chapter you can read about an unlucky scientist who really *did* lose his head. So just head over to the next page...

LUCKLESS LAVOISIER

Antoine Lavoisier might have "pinched" Scheele's discovery of oxygen, but by anyone's reckoning he was still a great scientist. And for much of his life he didn't seem too unlucky. He was rich and happy and successful. But then things went wrong.

Horribly wrong.

Horrible Science Hall of Fame: Antoine Lavoisier (1743-1794) NATIONALITY: French

Antoine's dad was a rich Paris lawyer and young Antoine got an excellent education in law (that was his dad's idea) and science (that was his real interest). He was also a member of the French Academy of Sciences and worked on boring projects such as a report on the Paris water supply. Bet that was dull as ditch water!

Creative chemistry

• In 1772 he found that all chemicals could exist as a gas, a liquid or a solid depending on how hot they were. Take water for example:

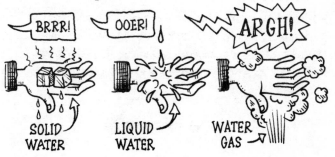

BRRR!

OOER!

ARGH!

SOLID WATER

LIQUID WATER

WATER GAS

115

- In the 1770s Lavoisier found that oxygen is needed for both rusting and burning. Chemists call the chemical reaction involved oxidation (ox-id-day-shun).
- He also showed that water is made up of oxygen and hydrogen. (Cavendish had already proved this but hadn't told anyone, remember?)
- Most important of all, Lavoisier insisted that all the chemicals he used should be carefully weighed and accurate records should be made of all his experiments.

Chemists hadn't always done this in the past. And this made it hard for other scientists to check to see whether that interesting brown liquid was the result of a new chemical reaction or simply the result of an embarrassing error.

Terror for tax takers

In 1768 Lavoisier became a tax collector in a private tax collecting company. Although the company was well run, the tax collectors weren't too popular. Well, it's not a very good way to make friends, and when revolution broke out in France the tax collectors were falsely accused of stealing public money. In 1793 Lavoisier was arrested and thrown into prison.

THIS IS VERY TAXING

Test your teacher

What else was Lavoisier accused of?

a) Forcing children to work as slave labour.

b) Adding dangerous chemicals to smoking tobacco and making people ill.

c) Using the French flag as a hankie when he had a bad cold.

IT'S RED, WHITE, BLUE... AND ER, GREEN

Answer: b) There wasn't an atom of proof for this charge, as Lavoisier might have said, but in 1793 people in France were being executed without proof all the time.

Antoine's wife, Marie-Anne, fought to save his life. She wrote to all Lavoisier's fellow scientists including Antoine Fourcroy (1755-1809).

Here's what she might have written:

31 December 1793
To Antoine Fourcroy

Dear Antoine

Please help me. I am begging you to save my husband. He is in prison after hiding in the Academy of Sciences. My husband is in terrible danger and all our money and all his scientific papers have been seized.

Antoine, you worked with my husband on chemistry experiments. You know very well he is no traitor. You know that he cared for the people and set up an experimental farm to improve farming and supported old age pensions and other ideas to help the poor. But I am rambling – it's only because I am so scared. Our only hope is if all the scientists in France protest to the government.

Can I count on your support?

Yours in desperation,
Marie-Anne Lavoisier

So what do you think Fourcroy did?
a) Protested strongly to the French government on behalf of his old friend.
b) Organized a protest march of scientists.
c) Nothing at all.

Answer: c) Fourcroy and the other French scientists didn't lift a finger. They knew that if they spoke out they too would be accused of plotting against the state.

On 7 May 1794 Lavoisier wrote a letter to Marie-Anne:

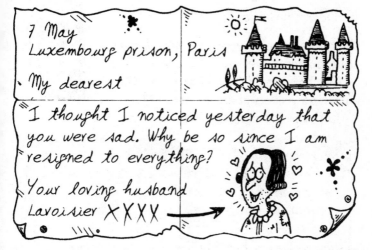

7 May
Luxembourg prison, Paris

My dearest

I thought I noticed yesterday that you were sad. Why be so since I am resigned to everything?

Your loving husband
Lavoisier XXXX

Then he wrote a more angry letter to his cousin: Augez de Villiers:

7 May
Luxembourg prison, Paris

Dear cousin

Rendering important services to one's country ... is not enough to preserve one from evil consequences and dying like a criminal. Farewell

Your cousin
Lavoisier

119

The following day Lavoisier was sentenced to death by the revolutionary court. That very afternoon the scientist and 27 other tax collectors were made to stand in open carts that trundled through the streets of Paris. Then they had to form an orderly queue as one by one they were strapped to a board and their heads were hacked off under the blood-stained blade of the guillotine. And all the time Lavoisier stayed brave and calm and comforted his friends until the last moment.

Two years later Lavoisier's body was dug up from its unmarked grave and given a decent burial. Fourcroy made a pompous tub-thumping speech:

Lavoisier was a martyr for science!

But Marie-Anne refused to speak to him. She never forgave Fourcroy and the other scientists who failed to save her husband. Meanwhile the science of chemistry that Lavoisier had done so much to develop moved on to new and exciting discoveries. As you can discover for yourself in the next chapter...

MODERN CHEMICAL MIXERS

If Lavoisier was to rise from his tomb and look round a modern chemistry lab he would be amazed. (But not half as amazed as the modern chemists would be to see Lavoisier – especially if he'd forgotten to put his head back on.)

In a modern lab, all the boring stuff like stirring chemicals for hours is done by robots. And substances can be heated very exactly using electric rings a bit like an electric cooker top but more sensitively controlled.

WHY CAN I SMELL SOUP AND NOT CHEMICALS, PERKINS?

SENSITIVE SCIENTIST

SENSITIVE CONTROLS

SOUP

The main achievements of chemists since Lavoiser's day are in two areas – understanding the elements and combining them to make useful new chemicals.

Braving the elements

By 1869 chemists had found lots more elements and it was all getting rather confusing. Then Russian scientist Dmitri Mendeleyev (1834-1907) found that you could group the elements in order of weight and how well they combined with other elements. The table Dimitri produced is known as the periodic table (that's table as in chart – not table as in wooden object with four legs). When Mendeleyev came to a gap in his table he boldly predicted that this was because the elements that should go there hadn't yet been discovered. And he was right – within a few years the missing elements were found.

As scientists learned more about atoms in the 1920s, (see page 23), they realized that for elements to combine together they need a complete set of electrons on the outermost layers of their atoms. To get this, atoms share or swap their electrons and bond together.

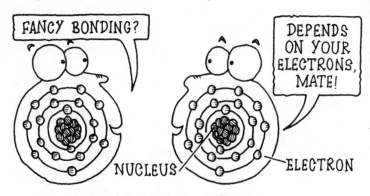

With this knowledge chemists can mix chemicals together and know which ones will join up. Modern chemists have cooked up a host of vital new substances such as plastics, including artificial fabrics such as nylon, and the Teflon that stops the remains of your dad's attempt to make rice pudding from sticking to pans.

Chemists have also done a lot of important work in biology. In the 1940s, for example, US chemist Linus Pauling, already an expert in how chemical reactions worked at an atomic level, figured out the shapes of proteins. These are chemicals made of thousands of atoms that are found in living things and the food that comes from living things such as milk and cheese. Proteins in your body perform vital tasks like building your muscles or as a part of chemicals called enzymes (en-zimes) that help you digest your food. Pauling encouraged many more chemists to work in this area – a new science known as biochemistry.

And talking about biology, read on for the low-down about suffering biologists...

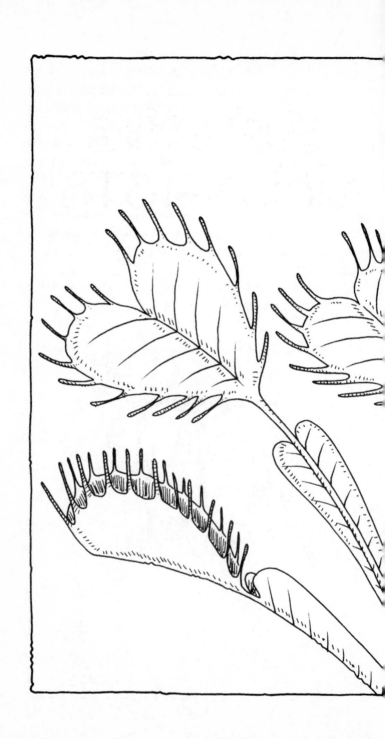

LEARNING FROM LIFE

Still wondering whether to be a scientist? Oh well, you don't have to make a final decision just yet. If you're into nature or fascinated with the incredible living machine known as your body you might want to be a biologist. Well, if so, a word of warning. Biologists in the past suffered just as much as any other scientists.

Our Stone Age pals the Ugs were interested in the world of plants and animals for one reason. No, they weren't into biology – they were after food. And they knew all about the creatures they hunted.

And, by trial and error, they must have found out quite early on which things were good to eat.

Since some plants and animals are poisonous you can be sure that some fatal mistakes were made along the way.

As you know, Aristotle pioneered a new way of studying nature by observation. (If you didn't know check back to page 30.) But oddly enough Aristotle's sensible ideas didn't properly catch on until the 1600s.

A boring historian says...

There is no simple explanation for this. People didn't travel much so they didn't see too many plants and animals from outside their area. And they already knew about the plants and animals of their own area ...

But things were about to change. In the 1500s Europeans began to explore the world. They saw strange plants and animals and brought them back home for study. A new science was being born and one of the earliest biologists was a courageous artist who had a thing about bugs. . .

MOSQUITO-BITTEN MARIA

Imagine you're eating a salad for your school dinner and you found that you were sharing your meal with a squirming green caterpillar. Would you...

a) turn green yourself and consider throwing up?

b) scoff the caterpillar with a dollop of tomato ketchup?

c) make a detailed drawing of the caterpillar to help scientists identify it?

Here's one person who would have definitely taken up option **c)** with enthusiasm.

Horrible Science Hall of Fame: Maria Merien
(1647-1717) NATIONALITY: Dutch

Maria was born in Germany where her dad made prints of flower drawings. When Maria was a baby her dad died and her mum married a Dutch flower painter named Jacob Marrell. Maria's mum obviously had a thing about artistic men who were into plants.

Maria's stepdad taught her to draw flowers and when she grew up she made a living painting silk with flower patterns. But soon she got interested in bugs like the caterpillars that sometimes turned up on the plants she painted. She even wrote a book full of tasteful drawings of insects in various stages of their development.

... AND UNFOLD YOUR WINGS. HOLD IT THERE, LOVELY!

Bugs are brilliant

Maria had married one of her stepdad's art pupils but in 1685 she left him and went to live in a religious commune. There she came across a gruesome collection of dead insects from Surinam in South America. Most of us would have said, "Yuck, I hope none of them are still alive," but Maria had never seen anything like it. She was fascinated by these strange and ugly creatures.

So Maria and her daughter Dorothy decided to go to Surinam and study bugs in the wild. This was an incredibly brave decision since it meant a hazardous voyage lasting several months with every danger of storms and pirate attack. And Surinam was known to be full of tropical diseases.

Bet you never knew!

Scientists often face danger when they go off to remote places in search of rocks or plants or animals to study. US Scientist Edward Cope (1840-1897) braved hostile natives when he toured the Midwest in search of fossil bones. But Edward refused to carry a gun to defend himself. Instead, when attacked by a hostile tribe he whipped out his false teeth. The shocked warriors went away. And that's the honest tooth – er, truth. Now back to Maria.

Here's what her letter home might have looked like.

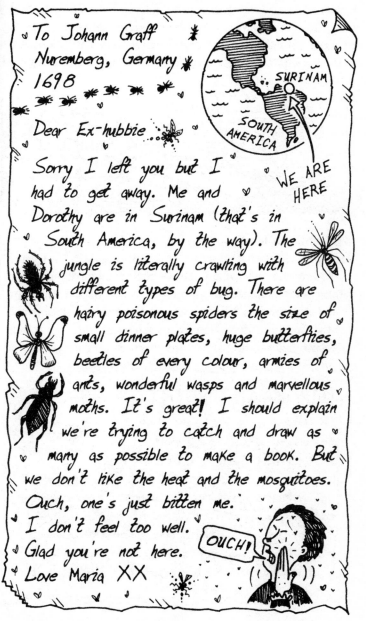

To Johann Graff
Nuremberg, Germany
1698

SURINAM

SOUTH AMERICA

Dear Ex-hubbie

WE ARE HERE

Sorry I left you but I had to get away. Me and Dorothy are in Surinam (that's in South America, by the way). The jungle is literally crawling with different types of bug. There are hairy poisonous spiders the size of small dinner plates, huge butterflies, beetles of every colour, armies of ants, wonderful wasps and marvellous moths. It's great! I should explain we're trying to catch and draw as many as possible to make a book. But we don't like the heat and the mosquitoes. Ouch, one's just bitten me. I don't feel too well. Glad you're not here. Love Maria XX

OUCH!

131

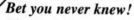

Bet you never knew!
The native guides Maria hired liked a joke. They used to stick two halves of different bugs together and claim they had found a new kind of insect. Maria innocently drew these revolting remains for her book.

GOSH! A GIANT SNAIL-BEE. THANK YOU!

Brilliant bug books

Maria fell ill with yellow fever – a disease she got from a mosquito bite in Surinam. Although she never regained her health she managed to publish a book of her Surinam insect drawings in 1705. It was a tremendous success and for the first time European insect scientists got a good look at weird and wonderful South American bugs.

IMPORTANT POINT
In the days before the camera was invented, scientists had to draw their experiments and results so other scientists could see what they were talking about. It's hard to imagine a scientist with a paintbrush or a pencil producing a pretty picture. But before photography they had to make the effort.

132

Bet you never knew!

Some of the strangest sights biologists found themselves drawing were the things they saw through their microscopes. This vital invention was made in about 1590, but the lenses and magnification were improved by Dutch scientist Anton van Leeuwenhoek (1632-1723). In 1676 he was looking at a scraping of smelly bits of rotten food from his teeth and saw tiny wriggling objects. They are the tiny living germs we now call bacteria.

But bacteria hide a deadly secret. A secret only uncovered in the nineteenth century. The key discoveries were made by a brilliant French couple.

A POWERFUL PARTNERSHIP

Marie and Louis Pasteur were a scientific couple. Although Louis normally gets most of the glory – his wife Marie was a vital helper in this work as the couple pushed themselves harder and harder to find the germs that caused disease.

Horrible Science Hall of Fame: Louis Pasteur (1822-1895) NATIONALITY: French

Young Louis didn't do brilliantly at school. But he really got into chemistry whilst studying to be a science teacher in Paris. And soon afterwards he made a great discovery...

Test your teacher

One day Pasteur rushed out of the lab shouting:

I have just made a great discovery ... I am so happy that I am shaking all over.

What had he found?

a) A sock that had gone missing one month ago.

b) That the structures of certain chemicals come in two forms that are mirror images of each other.

c) A previously unknown germ that causes warts.

Answer: b) This launched a new branch of science that uses light reflected from chemicals to study how the atoms in them are arranged.

Germ wars waged

But for Pasteur that was just the start. He took a series of jobs teaching science at French universities. And during his life he...

- Developed the theory that the bacteria we call germs cause disease. Before Pasteur, doctors believed that diseases were caused by bad smells.

Well, if you sniffed a blocked school toilet it would make you want to heave wouldn't it?

- Found out how to preserve wine by heating it to kill germs. This is the process now called pasteurization and it's what makes sure the milk for your cereal doesn't go sour – you'd be really sour if it did!
- Found the germs that caused lots of diseases such as anthrax (a very dangerous illness) and a disease of chickens called chicken cholera.
- Discovered how to weaken germs by heating them until they were damaged and could no longer multiply so fast. You could then inject them into a person. The weakened germs encourage the person to develop their body's defences against the disease. (This practice is called vaccination [vax-in-nay-shun]. In 1885 Pasteur saved the life of a boy called Joseph Meistner by injecting him with a vaccine against the killer disease rabies. The boy had been bitten by a dog that suffered from the disease.

Bet you never knew!

Louis and Marie Pasteur were married in 1849 shortly after he told her dad (a university principal) he had nothing to offer except his work. Marie wasn't put off. She wrote letters for her husband and helped with his experiments. But she once told her children:

Your father hardly speaks to me...

She added that that's how he'd always been.

An enormous error

Louis and Marie Pasteur were careful in their work and they made very few major errors. But in one experiment Louis missed a great opportunity ... here's what his lab notes might have looked like:

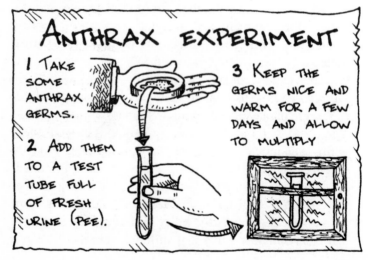

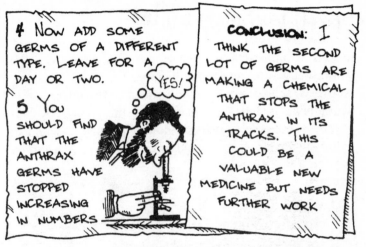

The Pasteurs never got round to it but today there is a whole class of medicines called antibiotics which are made from chemicals produced by fungi and the germs called bacteria. And these antibiotics kill germs like anthrax. The first antibiotic, penicillin, was discovered in 1928 by Scottish scientist Alexander Fleming (1881-1955).

At the age of 45 Louis Pasteur had a stroke. The brain seizure paralysed his left side. Despite this disability he carried on working with the help of Marie and his assistants. But not surprisingly, he became ever more bad-tempered. A second stroke in 1887 ended his scientific career.

At the same time, as biologists were delving ever deeper into the tiny world of bacteria, other scientists were speculating where life – not only tiny things, but all living things – came from and how it developed on planet Earth. The most famous was a quiet Englishman with a terrible tummy problem...

DITHERING DARWIN

In 1831 Charles Darwin set off on a voyage round the world that was to change the history of science. Now, any boring old science book will tell you that, but you probably won't learn that the commander on the *Beagle*, Robert Fitzroy (1805-1865), had his doubts about the scientist. Fitzroy, a great believer in judging a person's character by their bodily features, said:

I doubt whether Darwin has the determination to survive a difficult journey of several years... people with a broad, squat nose like his don't have the character.

Well, he did go and he just about had the character – as you're about to find out...

Horrible Science Hall of Fame: Charles Darwin (1809-1882) NATIONALITY: British

When he was a lad, young Charles enjoyed a joke. He once secretly picked a load of apples from a tree in the garden and then tried to kid his dad that he had found a store of "stolen" apples. His family didn't see the funny side and Darwin was packed off to school. Darwin's school teachers didn't think

138

much of him either. One teacher said:

The boy is entirely dull

When he grew up Darwin really didn't know what to do with his life. First he went to Edinburgh to study medicine. But he got upset at the sight of screaming patients being held down as surgeons performed bloody operations without painkillers.

PAINKILLERS HAVEN'T BEEN INVENTED YET SO YOU MAY FEEL A LITTLE SAW

So Darwin trained to be a clergyman. (At the time, many young men went into the Church as a profession.) But the lessons bored young Charles and he spent most of his time collecting beetles and butterflies. Then one of his friends told him about the *Beagle* voyage.

Test your teacher
1 What illness did Darwin suffer during the voyage?
a) Sea-sickness
b) Home-sickness
c) Mumps

2 How did Darwin catch the animals he studied?
a) He put glue on the ground and they stuck to it.

b) He made simple traps using branches and string.
c) He blasted them with a gun.

> **Answers: 1 a)** Darwin threw up for months. This must have made life pleasant for Fitzroy who had to share his cabin. (You can give your teacher half a mark for homesickness, because Darwin did miss home – but you should point out kindly that this is not generally considered an illness.)
> **2 c)** Darwin loved birds and small furry creatures. It's just that he also loved shooting them.

An evolving idea

99.9 per cent of science teachers will tell you that during the voyage Darwin began to think about how a species (type of animal) might change over time. This idea is now known as evolution.

Suffering scientists fact file

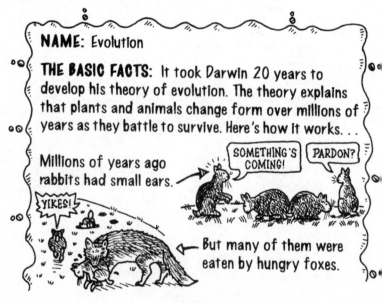

NAME: Evolution

THE BASIC FACTS: It took Darwin 20 years to develop his theory of evolution. The theory explains that plants and animals change form over millions of years as they battle to survive. Here's how it works...

Millions of years ago rabbits had small ears.

SOMETHING'S COMING!

PARDON?

YIKES!

But many of them were eaten by hungry foxes.

Some rabbits, with larger ears, heard the foxes sneaking up on them and escaped.

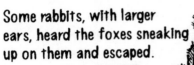

BYE!

YOU'VE GOT YOUR DAD'S EARS

The rabbits with larger ears survived to produce lots of baby bunnies and they had big ears too.

MUNCH!

CHOMP!

Eventually all rabbits had big ears.

THE SUFFERING DETAILS:

One of the famous examples of evolution at work are the tortoises of the Galapagos Islands in the Pacific.

SOUTH AMERICA

GALAPAGOS ISLANDS

Some shells have evolved to allow the tortoise to feed on higher plants.

Each island has a tortoise that evolved a slightly different shell. But Darwin didn't study the tortoises. He enjoyed eating them in soup. Would you do this to your pet tortoise?

Different shell shapes have evolved where tortoises feed on ground-level plants.

SOUP

141

Darwin dithers

Darwin dithered about going public on evolution because it was such a revolution in thinking. And he nearly left it too late. In June 1858 the postman delivered a letter that spoilt his entire day and nearly spoilt his entire life. It was only an article by another scientist, Alfred Russel Wallace (1823-1913), putting forward the same idea.

So the theory was announced at a meeting of scientists as a joint discovery although Darwin thought of it first.

Rotten rows

For most of his life Darwin suffered from a mysterious illness. Modern doctors aren't too sure what it was but the symptoms included throwing up every morning (for Darwin it must have been like his old seasickness) and embarrassing farting attacks. For this reason Darwin steered clear of the bitter public rows his theory provoked.

But you can't – so read on... You're bound to come across a few heated moments.

Many people felt Darwin's ideas clashed with the Bible story that God had created every type of animal. Worse still, Darwin's friends claimed that humans might have evolved from apes. In 1860 there was a famous debate in Oxford. 700 people turned up. The excitement was so great that one lady fainted.

The Bishop of Oxford made a speech attacking Darwin and asked one of Darwin's friends, Thomas Huxley (1825-1895), how he was descended from a monkey.

How would YOU reply?
a) At least I don't look like an ape – unlike you, gorilla features.
b) I believe we're all descended from ape-like creatures but evolution takes millions of years.
c) I would rather be related to an ape than to someone like you – a smart guy who uses his brains to twist the truth.

Answer: c)

A boring historian says...

Huxley put it in rather more elegant language but you get the general idea, and his reply caused a sensation. The bishop's big mistake was to spend most of his time attacking Darwin rather than discussing evolution. This gave the impression that the Bishop didn't know much about the theory he was supposed to be debating.

But in all the rows about the theory of evolution no one seemed to notice the biggest problem of all. Darwin said that young animals inherit their features from their parents but he didn't explain how this actually happened. He didn't explain because he didn't know. No one did. But an obscure monk was about to find out. Read on and you will too.

WHY DO I LOOK LIKE THIS, DAD?

I'M NOT SURE, SON. WE'D BETTER READ THE NEXT CHAPTER.

GROANING GREGOR

This is a story of a man who spent eight years of his life planting pea plants. And then everyone ignored his work. And after that I bet he got really p-e-e-e-ved and never touched mushy peas again.

Horrible Science Hall of Fame: Gregor Mendel (1822-1884)

NATIONALITY: Austrian

Gregor was born in Heizendorf (now in the Czech Republic). He was a serious boy who worked hard in school to get top marks and get to university. Too hard. Overwork made him ill – hope you don't have this problem!

BUT YOU NEVER DO ANY WORK SO HOW CAN IT MAKE YOU ILL?

JUST THINKING ABOUT IT, MISS!

So he decided to become a monk. He wasn't especially religious. But the peace and quiet would be ideal for scientific experiments.

Unfortunately his first job as a monk was visiting sick people. Softy Mendel couldn't bear seeing people suffer so the monks sent him to work as a teacher instead. Odd that – seeing as he couldn't stand suffering.

Gregor trained as a science teacher but failed his science exams. A few years later he tried again. But as he sat in the exam and looked at the hard questions he had a sudden and terrifying flashback. He KNEW that he would fail again. He felt sick with terror. His mind went blank and he burst into tears. Hope your science tests aren't quite this tough! Poor Gregor had to abandon the exam and gave up his studies.

But he didn't give up science altogether. He was breeding peas in the monastery gardens.

Dare you discover ... how to breed plants?
All you need is...
A flower such as a daffodil or a tulip.
A small artist's paint brush.

All you do is...
1 Lightly brush the anthers – these are the sticking-up bits on stalks that are arranged in a circle in the centre of the flower..

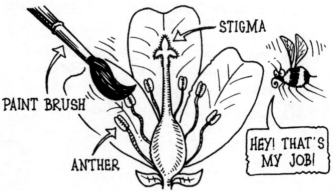

What do you notice?
a) The brush is moist.
b) The brush has gone green.
c) There is yellow dust on the brush.

Answer: c) The yellow stuff is pollen (that's the dusty stuff made by flowers that makes you sneeze). To breed plants you simply put it on the stigmas of another plant of the same type. The pollen grows a tube into the second plant and seeds form.

Mysterious messages

Mendel realized that the parent plants were passing on their features to their seedlings in the form of chemical messages (today we call them genes) in the pollen.

Suffering scientists fact file

NAME: Genes

THE BASIC FACTS: A gene is a chemical code that tells a plant or animal how to grow and develop. Living things get their genes from their parents. You got your genes from your parents and that's why you look like them. Note – that's genes NOT jeans (you'd look silly wearing your dad's baggy old jeans).

THE SUFFERING DETAILS: Now it gets complicated. You see, every living thing has TWO sets of genes – one from each parent. For example, Mendel's pea plants had two genes for growing. One said:

GROW SHORT **GS** and the other said: GROW TALL **GT**

But only one set of genes is switched on – so Mendel's pea plants were *either* short or tall.

By counting the different types of pea plant in each crop Mendel found that plants that carried the genes GROW SHORT and GROW TALL always grew tall.

I'LL CONTINUE THIS ON THE NEXT PAGE IN A MINUTE... I'M JUST GOING FOR A SHORT PEE.

147

> The only plants that grew short were those with the gene GROW SHORT and GROW SHORT. This was a dramatic discovery because it showed how genes work and some genes override others.
>
> GT + GT = TALL   GT + GS = TALL   GS + GS = SHORT

In all Mendel grew 28,000 pea plants. He studied their height, flower colour and five other characteristics. And he must have got really bored and tired sometimes because he said:

It requires ... some courage to undertake a labour of such far-reaching extent.

Well, courage, and a good supply of vapour rub for gardener's aches and pains. But Mendel had discovered the idea that plants (and animals) possess features that can be passed on to their descendants. This branch of biology is called genetics and neatly explains how evolution might work.

Miserable Mendel

Mendel felt really excited when in 1865 he proudly announced his discovery to a local science society. It was met with a spontaneous burst of ... APATHY. Feeling really discouraged, Mendel concentrated on his career as a monk. In 1868 he became the abbot – that's the top monk in his monastery. But in 1871 he got into an argument with the government over unpaid taxes. All this hassle made him ill and he died miserably in 1884.

Bet you never knew!
Scientists ignored Mendel's work until 1901 when three scientists working separately in Holland, Germany and Austria hit upon the same results. Then they found an article Mendel had written and realized that the monk had got there first. Not bad for someone who couldn't pass a science exam.

A deadly disagreement

Although today Mendel's ideas are generally accepted by scientists, there was one place where they were definitely rejected: Russia in the 1930s. And this had deadly results for a suffering Russian scientist.

RUSSIAN SCIENCE NEWS
1927

VAVILOV IS A HERO!

Plant breeder Nikolai Vavilov is a hero of our heroic people's revolution!

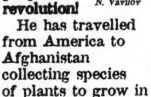

N. Vavilov

He has travelled from America to Afghanistan collecting species of plants to grow in Russia and feed our millions of workers and peasants. He and his staff have gathered over 30,000 plants for testing. And not only that! Vavilov has learnt how to breed new plants scientifically using the ideas of European scientists based on genetics. Russia salutes Comrade Vavilov!

RUSSIAN SCIENCE NEWS
1934

LYSENKO IS A HERO!

All hail to Comrade Trofim Lysenko who has shown that you can grow strong healthy wheat by cooling the wheat

T. Lysenko

seeds before sowing. So breeding new types of wheat is a waste of time. Genes don't exist! Comrade Lysenko (a good friend of our glorious and heroic leader Josef Stalin) is quite right to criticize the foreign ideas of that miserable traitor Vavilov!

RUSSIAN SCIENCE NEWS
1940

VAVILOV ARRESTED!

The traitor Nikolai Vavilov has been

arrested. We at the Russian Science News accuse Vavilov of causing the famines of the 1930s with his wicked foreign rubbish about plant breeding. Luckily we've got Stalin's friend, the wise and patriotic Trofim Lysenko, to show us how to grow more food.

STOP PRESS
We have just heard that Lysenko has been given a top job in the Academy of Sciences. Good for you, Trofim!

150

Vavilov's trial lasted a whole five minutes. The scientist was sent to a punishment camp in desolate Siberia. And there, three years later, the man who had devoted his entire life to feeding Russia starved to death. His enemy, Lysenko, became the top Russian scientist. But by the mid-1960s Lysenko's fellow scientists had turned against him and his views. In Russia Nikolai Vavilov is again honoured as a great scientist.

The reason why Lysenko was discredited lies in an amazing discovery by a group of young scientists in 1953. It was a discovery so huge and gigantic that even today it is leading to new breakthroughs.

So why not break through now to the next chapter?

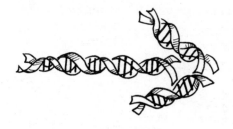

FORGOTTEN FRANKLIN

This is a story about four scientists and one awesome discovery which was to change the way we look at the world for ever. Three of the scientists achieved fame and fortune, but one of them, Rosalind Franklin, is almost forgotten. This chapter is mainly her story.

Horrible Science Hall of Fame: Rosalind Franklin (1920-1958) NATIONALITY: British

During the Second World War the young scientist researched coal. Now, of course, you or I might say...

But Rosie did much more. She showed that coal could be made into a new material called carbon fibre. Nowadays carbon fibre is used to strengthen plastic to make a light substance that is tougher than steel. And you'll find carbon fibre in planes and cars and even tennis rackets.

But carbon fibre wasn't Rosie's greatest work...

Crucial crystals

Her real interest was in using X-rays to study the structure of the atoms in crystals. By looking at the pattern of reflected X-rays you can tell a lot about how the atoms are arranged. She did this work in Paris and then King's College, London. In 1951 she was working on a chemical called DNA and that's when the trouble began...

Suffering scientists fact file

NAME: DNA (deoxyribose nucleic acid)
If you want to show off, learn to say it:

de-oxy-ri-boze new-klee-ic acid

THE BASIC FACTS: This is a substance mainly found in the nucleus (new-klee-us) of living cells and by 1951 it was known to be the stuff that genes are made of.

CELL

NUCLEUS

SEVERAL LENGTHS OF DNA ARE CONTAINED WITHIN THE NUCLEUS

GENES ARE FOUND WITHIN THE DNA

YOU WILL INHERIT GENES FROM YOUR FATHER AND MOTHER

THE SUFFERING DETAILS:
DNA is awesomely complicated. It contains about ten million atoms so it's a bit of a job to find out how they're all put together.

Over the page is what Rosalind's secret diary might have looked like. (OK, it probably didn't, but it might have.)

JULY 1951

Dear diary

I'm so miserable. Here I am at King's College studying DNA and I ought to be really happy. But I'm not. There's a guy here called Maurice Wilkins and he's doing the same job as me. But I can't get on with him. OK, to be fair he can't get on with me and we argue all the time, it's awful. At least I'm making progress with my work. I've designed a new X-ray camera which takes clearer pictures and I reckon DNA looks like a corkscrew. But it's hard to make out.

NOVEMBER 1951

Today a young American turned up at a lecture I was giving about my work. He was a skinny lad with a bit of a quiff and a turned up nose. He said his name was James Watson. Well, it looks like this Watson and his pal Francis Crick are working on DNA too, and they're mates of the dreaded Wilkins. They've not got anywhere though. During my lecture Watson just sat there looking gob-smacked and drank it all in. He didn't even bother to make notes.

MARCH 1952

Wilkins and I went to Cambridge to look at Watson's model of DNA. I met Crick there too. He's balding and very clever and talks fast but I didn't like him for some reason. Anyway, the model was TERRIBLE. It was shaped like three corkscrews intertwined. Huh - well, I put them right. You should have seen Watson's face!

JANUARY 1953

rubbish! →

My work is making good progress and some time in the next few years I will make a breakthrough. Funny thing is, one of my best X-ray pictures of DNA has gone missing. I wonder whether Wilkins has borrowed it. Wouldn't put it past him to take it without asking.

Maurice Wilkins had indeed borrowed the picture and he had shown it to his pals Watson and Crick.

A boring historian says...

This is just ONE version of what happened. Many historians disagree, saying that Wilkins showed his friends some of his own pictures but not one of Rosie's.

A tremendous team

James Watson and Francis Crick made a perfect team. Crick later wrote:

Jim and I hit it off ... because a certain youthful arrogance ... and an impatience with sloppy thinking were natural to us.

Crick was an expert in Rosalind's field of X-ray crystal studies and Watson had studied DNA in types of tiny germs called viruses. And they were well-matched in other ways. Whilst Rosalind patiently plodded on with her work, Watson and Crick enjoyed relaxing and chatting. Is this your ideal approach to science too? Well, don't get over-excited – Watson and Crick did work very hard, when they were in the mood.

When they saw the crucial X-ray picture they knew at once that DNA was shaped like a twisted ladder with pairs of chemicals forming the rungs.

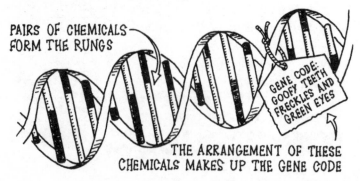

PAIRS OF CHEMICALS FORM THE RUNGS

GENE CODE: GOOFY TEETH FRECKLES AND GREEN EYES

THE ARRANGEMENT OF THESE CHEMICALS MAKES UP THE GENE CODE

Watson set out to build a model using bits of old wire and cardboard and beads. Together they had cracked the mystery of DNA with perhaps a bit of help from Rosalind Franklin.

Dynamic DNA

The discovery of the structure of DNA was a vital breakthrough. Everyone has a unique DNA code in their cells and today scientists can use bits of DNA in skin and spit left at crime scenes to identify criminals. Throughout the world police forces are setting up databases of the DNA of criminals so they can be checked up if their DNA is ever found at a crime scene.

In 1988 scientists set about mapping every one of the 100,000 genes that make up a human.

By 1997 they had found the areas of DNA linked to 450 diseases caused by the faulty copying of genes within the cells of the body. One such disease is cystic fibrosis (sis-tic fi-bro-sis) which attacks the lungs.

Bet you never knew!

1 At the end of the 1990s scientists developed a spray to help fight cystic fibrosis. A patient suffering from the disease breathes in the spray containing healthy genes to replace their damaged genes. The spray helps the genes to travel to the patient's lungs.

2 And it's now possible to test a person's genes to find out whether the genes are damaged. If they are, this could cause a deadly disease in the future. Obviously if the disease is one that could be treated this would be a vital warning, but what if the disease can't be treated? Chances are the person wouldn't exactly be desperate to hear the horrible news. What would you choose?

New life forms

And DNA technology has made it possible for scientists to shuffle the genes in DNA to make new forms of life. For example...

- Microbes that make a chemical called rennin that is used to curdle cheese. Sounds disgusting? Well, the only other source of rennin is the juice from a calf's stomach – yuck!

THAT'S GOOD "MOOS" FOR US

- New kinds of plants that don't get killed by plant disease or weedkillers. Many people are worried about whether such genetically modified (GM) foods are safe to eat or whether they might damage our health or the environment in some way.

- Microbes that make a vital chemical called insulin. People who suffer from the disease diabetes need to take this chemical so that sugar doesn't build up in their bloodstream. And more life-forms are being developed every year.

Test your teacher

Rosalind never found out whether her picture had made Watson and Crick's breakthrough possible. But surely she deserved some reward for her work. What do you think she got?

a) A share in the Nobel Prize.

b) The whole prize to herself.

c) Not a bean.

> **Answer: c)** Rosalind died young in 1958 and the Nobel Prize wasn't awarded until 1962. The prize was shared by Watson, Crick and Wilkins. The rules said that you can't give a Nobel Prize to a dead person. Well, I suppose it would be quite hard for a dead person to collect their award in person.

Meanwhile, elsewhere in biology, scientists are making discoveries and getting into huge arguments about them. So read on and hopefully you won't get too hot under the collar...

MODERN LIFE SCIENTISTS

Although Mendel's work and the subsequent discovery of genes had helped to show how evolution takes place, scientists are still arguing about the details of the subject. After all, they're hard to prove. Well, you could set up an experiment using a group of animals to see how they evolve, but you'd then have to wait over a million years to test the result.

It's clear from studying fossils that every 26 million years or so much of life on Earth is wiped out. It happened to the dinosaurs, but cheer up it probably won't happen to us for millions of years. This might be caused by comets hitting the Earth or giant volcanic eruptions or both. Anyway, some scientists think that these mass extinctions gave the surviving creatures a chance to evolve more quickly because there was less competition for food and living space. But some scientists disagree because they have studied fossils that seem to show that evolution is more gradual.

Mind you, just because we weren't hit by a comet this weekend doesn't mean that plants and animals aren't dying out. They are, and who's to blame? We are. Humans are destroying rainforests and coral reefs and other places rich in plant and animal life at a scary rate. In fact, all the time types of plants and animals are dying out.

Bet you never knew!

One of the first people to blow the whistle on what was going on was US scientist Rachel Carson (1907-1964). In 1962 she wrote a book showing the damage done to birds by DDT, a chemical used to kill insects. DDT has saved about five million human lives and won Paul Müller (1899-1965), the Swiss scientist who developed it, the Nobel Prize in 1948. But it's now widely banned because of the damage it can do to other species.

Meanwhile not everyone is thrilled about altering the genes of plants and animals. Although many people believe that the technology is generally safe, in 1999 newspaper reports claimed that rats that ate a type of genetically altered potato seemed to be less able to fight off disease.

Scientists agreed that the experiments the reports were based on didn't prove anything very much because of the way they were carried out. (Even scientists get it wrong sometimes.) Many people think we need more tests before genetically modified food can be declared safe – so the subject remains a hot potato.

So what will you be? A brave biologist warning the world about the dangers it faces by wiping out plants and animals? Or will you be a physicist? Someone who gets to grips with the really deep fundamentals of the Universe. Whilst you're deciding, let's get back to basics.

PHYSICAL FACTFINDERS

Back in the Stone Age, the Ugs were even less interested in physics than the average child at school. Don't forget their chief concern was how to get food. But although they didn't realize it, they were still making use of physics...

NOW, SON, I'VE OFTEN WISHED THAT MY SPEAR WAS, WELL ... JUST A BIT LONGER. GETTING TOO CLOSE TO AN ENRAGED MAMMOTH CAN REALLY SPOIL MY DAY.

ANYWAY, I'VE INVENTED SOMETHING TO MAKE LIFE EASIER. I'M CALLING IT A BOW AND ARROW. IT'S BASICALLY SOME NICE TOUGH MAMMOTH GUT TIED TO SOME BENDY WOOD.

AND I CAN FIRE THIS ROCK – THAT'S THE ARROW, LIKE THIS ...

YEAH IT STILL NEEDS A BIT OF WORK.

WHY NOT USE A LITTLE SPEAR?

A boring scientist says...

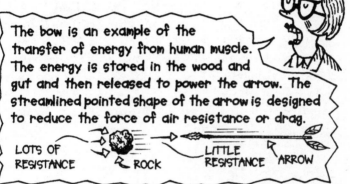

The bow is an example of the transfer of energy from human muscle. The energy is stored in the wood and gut and then released to power the arrow. The streamlined pointed shape of the arrow is designed to reduce the force of air resistance or drag.

LOTS OF RESISTANCE — ROCK — LITTLE RESISTANCE — ARROW

But of course, no one realized this because physics as a science hadn't been invented yet. You'll remember how Aristotle made quite a few mistakes in physics but that his views held sway until Galileo started to come up with something better. (Check out pages 30 and 74 if you don't remember.) Anyway, eventually the science of physics received its biggest boost ever from a person who was a scientific megastar and an incredible personality. Incredibly clever, incredibly rude, incredibly nasty.

Are you ready to meet him?

CLUE

INCREDIBLE ISAAC

Isaac Newton was so famous in his lifetime that French noble the Marquis de l'Hôpital wondered whether he might actually be a god:

> I picture him to myself as a celestial genius

Most modern scientists agree that he was the greatest scientist who ever lived. So what made him so incredible?

Horrible Science Hall of Fame: Isaac Newton (1642-1727) NATIONALITY: English

When he was a lad Isaac wrote a list of all the things he had done wrong. Not something most of us would do, but it takes all sorts. Here is an extract. We've added two things which Newton didn't confess to – can you work out which ones are false?

I CONFESS, BY ISAAC NEWTON (AGED 17):
1. I PUNCHED MY SISTER.
2. I WANTED TO BURN DOWN THE HOUSE WITH MY STEP DAD IN IT.
3. I PERFORMED A CRUEL EXPERIMENT ON MY PET HAMSTER.
4. I STOLE AN APPLE FROM MY FRIEND.
5. I STARTED A UFO SCARE.

A star student

Most of Newton's discoveries were made when he was
studying at Cambridge University in the 1660s. At this
point he was very poor and had to work as a kind of servant
running errands and even emptying his teacher's chamber
pots. (There weren't proper toilets in the college rooms and
people had to poo in the pots. Would *you* volunteer to
empty your teacher's potty?)

As people realized how clever he was Newton rose to
become professor of Mathematics at Cambridge and later
worked for the Royal Mint where England's coins were
made. Between 1689 and 1690 he was a Member of
Parliament but he only ever spoke once and that was to ask
someone to open a window. Anyway here's a quick run
down of the great man's achievements…

Newton's claims to fame

1665: Newton began to develop the mathematical system now called calculus. This allows scientists to calculate constantly varying quantities, for example the shifting load on a bridge.

1664-1666: He discovered that light is made up of different colours. He did this by passing sunlight through a glass shape called a prism that split the light into colours.

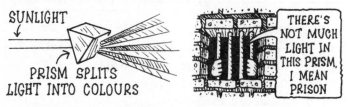

SUNLIGHT

PRISM SPLITS
LIGHT INTO COLOURS

THERE'S NOT MUCH LIGHT IN THIS PRISM, I MEAN PRISON

1666: He began to develop the theory of gravity.

1687: Newton's greatest achievement was to write a book on gravity and the laws that make objects move. The *Principia,* as it was called, was one of the most famous science books ever – not to mention one of the most expensive books you can buy today!

Newton and the balloon

Here is another first for *Horrible Science.* The one and only Sir Isaac Newton has agreed to demonstrate his laws of motion using this balloon.

My action is blowing this balloon up

Law 1 says every action has an equal and opposite reaction. So that when I let the balloon go, the opposite reaction of the balloon pushing against the air inside will push air out of the opening and send the balloon flying off in the other direction.

Law 2 – the acceleration of the balloon depends on the force acting on it and its mass.*

* That's the posh word for the amount of matter in an object.

Law 3 – unless the forces acting on the balloon change or another force gets in the way, the balloon will continue to move at a constant speed.

The force of gravity has pulled the balloon to the ground.

Anyway, **Law 3** also says that now the balloon has stopped moving it will stay still until another force makes it move.

At this point Newton began to explain the mathematical basis of his laws but we thanked him and made our excuses. The wonderful thing about Newton's work is that it doesn't just work for balloons. The laws explain EVERYTHING (well, apart from those flippin' atoms!). But from squids to space rockets, to snot flying out of your nostrils when you sneeze, everything moves in a scientifically predictable way.

And Newton's ideas are still used today to design new kinds of cars or to explain how bridges sway about in high winds. They even explain how rockets and jet planes work.

Got all that?

Well, did you understand it?

Although Newton's *Principia* was a brilliant work of science it was so full of complex maths that only a few people could understand it. A nobleman actually offered £500 to anyone who could explain what the book was about – but there were no takers. Another frustrated reader pointed at Newton in the street saying:

There goes a man that has written a book that neither he nor anyone else understands.

Actually, Newton knew very well. But he said that he had made it hard to understand because he didn't want to be bothered by stupid questions from non-scientists. Charming!

Basic blunders

Actually, Newton wasn't right about absolutely everything. Here is something he got wrong:

Light travels through water faster than empty space.

A boring scientist says...

Wrong – light travels 33 per cent faster through space because there are no atoms to get in the way.

Moreover, Newton spent loads of money and many years in futile experiments based on alchemy. Yes, he honestly believed you could make gold from other metals. In fact, he was so keen on this idea that he used to sleep in his lab for six weeks at a time – would you do this in your school lab? When he was awake he was working on experiments that involved melting different kinds of metals together and got absolutely nowhere.

Antisocial Isaac

For all his genius, Newton was a miserable man. He was only ever known to have laughed once in his entire life. One of his few friends once told him that he couldn't see the point of studying the work of Euclid the inventor of geometry. Isaac burst into merry peals of laughter.

Anyone see the joke here?

Naturally, being such a massive celeb you might imagine that Newton enjoyed giving press interviews, signing autographs and getting letters from his adoring fans. But you'd be wrong. Newton seemed to enjoy being nasty and antisocial. He once wrote an odd letter to another rare friend, Samuel Pepys (1633-1703):

Dear Samuel
I must withdraw from your acquaintance and see neither you nor the rest of my friends any more.
Yours, Isaac

No one knows why Newton wrote this and he was back in touch within a year. But although he lived to a great age he never repeated the brilliant scientific achievements of his younger years.

There was just one place where Newton felt comfortable, and that – surprise, surprise – was in meetings of a scientific club. In 1702 Newton became President of the Royal Society, the oldest and poshest British scientific society.

Newton had really opened the subject of physics up to other scientists. And in this work on gravity he had described a vital force that shapes the universe. But there is another force, the force that flows out of your power plugs every time you flick a switch. To discover more about the scientist who helped to explain it, why not switch to the next page.

You could be in for a shock...

ELECTRIFYING FARADAY

Told you.

Remember Thales rubbing amber to make static electricity? Remember van Mussenbroek's assistant getting a nasty shock from the electrically-charged bowl of water? Well, eighteenth- and early nineteenth-century physicists were investigating electricity.

For example, Italian scientist Alessandro Volta (1745-1827) had built a simple battery. And at that moment in England a young scientific genius was busy delivering newspapers and feeling desperately hungry. But when he grew up he would electrify science. He was:

Horrible Science Hall of Fame: Michael Faraday (1791-1867) NATIONALITY: English

Michael's dad was a blacksmith who spent most of Michael's childhood in bed and ill. Michael's family was so poor that they went short of food and had to beg for help from the local workhouse. The boy had little schooling and at the age of 13 he went to work for a bookseller and learnt how to bind books.

One day Michael was binding a book called *Conversations about Chemistry* by popular science writer Jane Marcet (1769-1858). The book tells the story of two girls, Emily and Caroline, and their science teacher, Mrs Robson. Emily is quiet and serious but Caroline likes exciting experiments and explosions – know anyone like that? Michael found the book so fascinating he enrolled in a local science club and then a friendly customer gave him tickets to the Royal Institution lectures.

IMPORTANT POINT

As science became more complicated it grew harder for non-scientists to understand new discoveries. People like Jane Marcet played a vital role by writing science books for the general public. Science clubs and the Royal Institution (founded 1799) organized science lectures to highlight the latest developments.

Michael was bowled over by the Royal Institution. Just imagine watching your fave football stars or pop singers. He sat entranced in one of the comfy blue seats as top scientist Sir Humphry Davy (1778-1829) lectured on science. "One day," thought Michael, "that could be me on stage." He longed to work at the Royal Institution.

CAN YOU SPOT M.F. IN THE CROWD?

He made detailed notes on all the lectures. And afterwards he copied them out in his best handwriting and drew and then coloured in pictures of the experiments. Then he bound the work in a fine leather binding. (Could you do homework like this?) Michael sent his work to Sir Joseph Banks (1744-1820), the President of the Royal Institution, with a polite note asking for a job.

Sir Joseph didn't bother to reply.

FARADAY'S LETTER MIGHT HAVE LOOKED LIKE THIS

Dear Sir Joseph
I enclose a pressy for you.
Can I have a job, please?
Best wishes
Michael Faraday

SIR J.B.'S LETTER DEFINITELY LOOKED LIKE THIS

What would you do?

Burst into tears and give up?

Michael didn't. He was determined to get that job. So he made another beautiful hand-coloured book and sent it to Sir Humphry Davy. Sir Humphry told him to stick to binding books.

But then Faraday's luck changed.

Davy's assistant got sacked for fighting and the scientist managed to blind himself temporarily in a dangerous chemistry experiment. And because he was in need of help, young Michael was given a job that paid even less than the pittance he earned as a bookbinder. Michael didn't care – he loved the work. He happily washed nasty smelly test-tubes and ran errands and swept up. Then he began to help with experiments, and in 1814 Davy took him on a grand tour of Europe. But it was nearly a disaster.

They met leading scientists and everything would have been fine if it hadn't have been for Lady Davy. Michael had a terrible temper and Lady Davy wound him up something rotten. Michael had to bottle up his rage. Here's one of his letters...

To Benjamin Abbot
Rome
January 25 1815

Dear Ben

I should have but little to complain of if I were travelling with Sir Humphry alone or were Lady Davy like him, but ... she is ... proud to an excessive degree and delights in making her inferiors feel her power.

Yours miserably,
                    Michael

Lady D

And here's how Lady Davy may have seen things. (OK, she probably didn't put it in quite this way.)

Geneva 1815

Dear Diary

That jumped up Faraday is ruining my holiday. He seems to think he's more than just a servant. Oh dear - the effrontery! We went to dinner with

flamin' Faraday

> Professor de la Rive and we found he'd set a place for Faraday at *our* table and not with the other servants. Well, I had to make a scene as it's not the done thing. But, oh dear, I'm afraid these scientists don't understand etiquette. The Professor allowed Faraday to dine at a separate table - but not with the other servants. I was fuming but Sir Humphrey did nothing - as usual..

When Faraday became better known as a scientist he was elected to the Royal Society. And in 1825 he took over Davy's job at the Royal Institution. His dream had come true and the rich and famous flocked to his lectures. The days when he was a mere "servant" were long forgotten.

Faraday's famous findings

In 1825 he discovered benzene (that vital industrial chemical) when looking at the ingredients of the smelly, greasy oil found in a dead whale. (I bet he had a whale of a time.) But today Faraday is most famous for his work on electricity...

177

Suffering scientists fact file

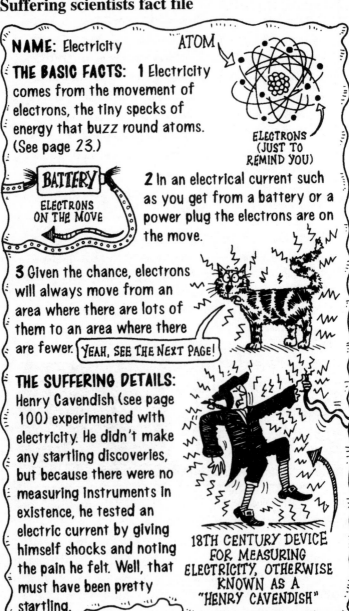

NAME: Electricity

ATOM

THE BASIC FACTS: **1** Electricity comes from the movement of electrons, the tiny specks of energy that buzz round atoms. (See page 23.)

ELECTRONS (JUST TO REMIND YOU)

BATTERY
ELECTRONS ON THE MOVE

2 In an electrical current such as you get from a battery or a power plug the electrons are on the move.

3 Given the chance, electrons will always move from an area where there are lots of them to an area where there are fewer. YEAH, SEE THE NEXT PAGE!

THE SUFFERING DETAILS: Henry Cavendish (see page 100) experimented with electricity. He didn't make any startling discoveries, but because there were no measuring instruments in existence, he tested an electric current by giving himself shocks and noting the pain he felt. Well, that must have been pretty startling.

18TH CENTURY DEVICE FOR MEASURING ELECTRICITY, OTHERWISE KNOWN AS A "HENRY CAVENDISH"

Dare you discover (1) ... how to see electricity?

All you need is...
A cat (or any other furry object)
Cold dry weather
A piece of nylon

All you do is...
1 Darken the room or wait until it gets dark.
2 Stroke the cat with the nylon.

What do you notice?
a) The cat begins to glow in the dark.
b) I see tiny sparks.
c) I could just hear a few very faint clicks.

Answer: b) By stroking Tiddles you removed electrons from the surface of her fur. But electrons always go to areas where there are fewer of them – remember? So what you are seeing and hearing is billions of electrons leaping from the nylon back to Tiddles' fur.

YOU TURN THE LIGHTS OUT AND START RUBBING ME WITH A CLOTH ... WHAT THE HECK'S GOING ON?

Dare you discover (2) ... how electricity can make things move?

All you need is...
Yourself
A woollen sweater
A balloon
A thread 10 centimetres (4 inches) long

All you do is...
1 Put on the sweater.
2 Blow up the balloon and tie its end.
3 Tie the thread to the end of the balloon.
4 Rub the balloon on your sweater a few times.
5 Hold the thread so the balloon hangs down a few centimetres away from you.

What do you notice?
a) The balloon moves towards me.
b) The balloon seems to swing away from me.
c) The balloon produces sparks and an alarming crackling noise.

> **Answer: a)** The balloon picks up electrons from the sweater but the electrons pull the balloon back to the sweater because this now has fewer electrons.

Electrifying discoveries

In 1832 Faraday found that an electric current can separate chemicals in liquid. This process, now known as electrolysis (el-leck-trol-lo-sis), is useful for plating cutlery with a thin coat of silver. But his greatest discovery was made the year before.

In 1831 he built the world's first dynamo to produce an electric current. Faraday had found in 1821 that a moving magnet produces an electric current in a wire. The magnetic force is made by electrons spinning inside the magnet and the force they produce affects the electrons in the wire and starts them moving. (In fact scientists view them as the same force because an electrical current will always give out a magnetic force too. The name of this force is electro-magnetism.)

Ten years later Faraday returned to the work and found that you can move the metal wire and keep the magnet in one place and still make a current. Here is Faraday proudly showing off his new invention...

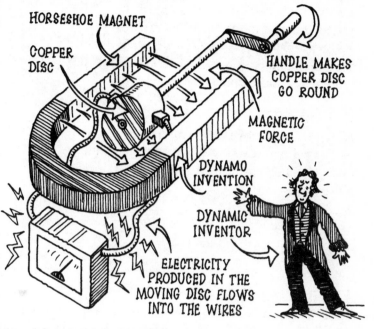

HORSESHOE MAGNET

COPPER DISC

HANDLE MAKES COPPER DISC GO ROUND

MAGNETIC FORCE

DYNAMO INVENTION

DYNAMIC INVENTOR

ELECTRICITY PRODUCED IN THE MOVING DISC FLOWS INTO THE WIRES

A gigantic discovery

This discovery is so huge that it would take an entire book to get through all the effects that it has had on our lives. Basically, without the power of electricity every machine that uses electricity wouldn't exist. Have you ever been stuck in the middle of a massive power cut?

Back to the dark ages

No, it's not my idea of FUN either (at least you can read this book, so cheer up). But it all goes to show how vital Faraday's discovery really was.

IMPORTANT POINT

Across the Atlantic, US scientist Joseph Henry (1797-1878) was making the same discovery. In fact, Henry actually made it in 1830 but the British scientist got the credit because he published his results first. It's a good example of how scientists often make the same discoveries at the same time.

YEE HAR! I'VE DONE IT!

GOOD SHOW! SUCCESS AT LAST!

Bet you never knew!

In one dramatic demonstration Faraday built a wooden cage 3.66 metres (12 feet) square and covered it in metal foil and wire. The scientist stood inside the cage and an assistant ran 100,000 volts of electricity through the bars. Sparks flew from the cage and if Faraday had touched the bars he would have been killed instantly. Any volunteers for this experiment?

Classic classes

Does your teacher deliver brilliant lessons that fill the entire class with excitement and a desire to learn more? Well, here's your chance to see how they measure up against the best and the worst science teachers ever. As you might have realized, Michael Faraday was one of the greatest. He even employed a teacher of elocution (correct speech) to attend his lectures. The teacher held up cards telling Faraday when he was speaking too fast or too slow. Would you be brave enough to do this to your science teacher?

Teaching disasters

One evening in 1827, British scientist Charles Wheatstone (1802-1875) was due to lecture at the Royal Institution. The young scientist was chewing his lip and pacing up and down and getting more and more nervous. Then, in the lecture before Wheatstone's, a mummified cat was cut open. Yuck! The grisly sight was the final straw. The scientist ran away. Since then, lecturers at the Royal Institution have been locked in the building.

The next chapter is about a terrible teacher too. This famous physicist tended to mumble and use jargon that few people could understand. But if he was a useless teacher, he was a marvellous scientist. And his name..?

Well, turn over the page and all will be revealed.

MARVELLOUS MAXWELL

Scottish scientist James Clerk Maxwell was undoubtedly a genius and even at school he was regarded as uncommonly bright. It was a real pity that he had to wear that frilly shirt...

Horrible Science Hall of Fame: James Clerk Maxwell (1831-1879) NATIONALITY: Scottish

Even as a wee lad young James was into science. At the age of two he asked his mum where streams came from and how locks worked and other questions that she couldn't answer. Maybe James got his curiosity from his inventor dad. Maxwell senior also liked designing clothes and this proved a problem. Would you like to turn up at school looking like this?

James Maxwell's first day at school

SPEAKING WITH A STRONG COUNTRY ACCENT WHICH SOUNDED ODD TO THE OTHER CHILDREN AND A STAMMER THAT NO ONE COULD UNDERSTAND

OCH AYE THE N,N,N, N,N,N,NOO

EMBARRASSING FRILLY SHIRT MADE BY HIS AUNT

THICK ITCHY WOOLLEN JACKET DESIGNED BY HIS DAD

SCRAP MATERIALS FOR SCIENCE EXPERIMENTS

DEAD BEETLE COLLECTION

SQUARE-TOED SHOES MADE BY HIS DAD

No wonder the other kids picked on him and called young James "Daftie". But he wasn't daft – far from it. At the age of 14 he wrote his first science article (on how to draw an ellipse – that's a kind of flattened circle, remember?) and he spent most of the rest of his life as a university professor in Scotland and Cambridge.

More school problems

Maxwell wasn't the only scientist to have problems at school. Just take a look at this lot:

- Carl Linnaeus (1707-1778), the Swedish biologist who developed the system of Latin names now used to identify plants and animals, nonetheless hated Latin at school. His teacher told his dad:

Your son ought to become a cobbler.

Presumably the teacher thought that people who mend shoes don't need brains – which is a load of old cobblers.

- William Bateson (1861-1926) was a distinguished British geneticist, (that's someone who studies genetics, the science that Mendel helped to launch). But when he was at school his teacher had described him as:

A vague and aimless boy.

187

That didn't stop Bateson getting a first-class science degree.

• Mega-genius Albert Einstein hated school. The teaching involved lots of tests and learning boring facts off by heart and discipline was strict. Albert later said:

> It is nothing short of a miracle that modern methods of education have not ... strangled the sacred spirit of curiosity.

Try that one on your science teacher ... if you dare!

Bet you never knew!
Scientists also suffered the brutal conditions endured by many children in schools. For example, the inventor of the bouncing bomb that was used to destroy German dams in 1943, Neville Barnes Wallis (1887-1979), had to sleep on a bare wooden bed and play rugby on a concrete pitch. And I bet he didn't bounce too much when he fell on it. Now back to Maxwell.

A quick quiz

As a young student James Clerk Maxwell had some strange hobbies. Can you decide which were the two pastimes he enjoyed from this list?

a) Spray-painting scientific calculations on the walls.

b) Running around the house at 2 a.m. and waking everyone up.

c) Flicking chewing gum so that it stuck to the back of his

teacher's head and then blaming someone else.
d) Throwing a cat from his bedroom window.
e) Allowing a snake to escape down the toilet and then trying to find it in the sewers.

Answer: b) According to one fellow student he enjoyed running past their doors at two in the morning. He annoyed everyone...

... until the inhabitants of the rooms along his track got up to have shots at him with boots, hairbrushes, etc., as he passed.

And **d)** Maxwell wanted to throw the cat in such a way that it couldn't land on its feet. He succeeded, apparently, but in later life he denied doing it. Well he would, wouldn't he? How many famous scientists would admit cruelty to harmless little pussy cats?

☠ HORRIBLE HEALTH WARNING!

We have feelings too, so don't even think about copying Maxwell.
If you do you will probably have to eat up any spare tins of cat food ... which would serve you right.

Maxwell's dramatic discoveries

Maxwell made loads of discoveries. For example, in 1860 he used maths to show that heat is really the movement of molecules. But his very greatest achievement came in 1864. Using little more than a notebook, a pencil and his brilliant brain, he drew up a series of mathematical rules (equations) that govern the behaviour of electricity.

This sounds a bit boring – but it had elephant-sized implications. Maxwell realized that these equations meant:

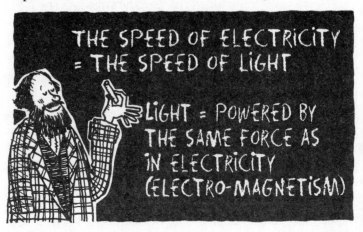

THE SPEED OF ELECTRICITY = THE SPEED OF LIGHT

LIGHT = POWERED BY THE SAME FORCE AS IN ELECTRICITY (ELECTRO-MAGNETISM)

And Maxwell guessed that other rays similar to light might be produced, although they may be ones we can't see.

A boring scientist says...

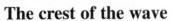

Maxwell was right, right and right again!

The crest of the wave

In 1888 German Heinrich Hertz (1857-1894) discovered radio waves – the first of Maxwell's invisible rays. Just think – thanks to Maxwell's work scientists were able to develop radios and TVs. After all, radios use radio waves and TV signals are radio waves too.

Then in 1895 another German scientist, Wilhelm Röntgen (1845-1923), discovered a new set of waves – X-rays, which were invisible like radio waves, but had far more energy. X-rays shine through skin but not more solid objects such as bones, so you can have an X-ray and see your own bones. And X-rays are also used in airports to find bombs and weapons hidden in luggage.

So Maxwell's equations changed the world. Not bad for someone they called "Daftie", armed only with a notebook and pencil. But Maxwell wasn't always right – thank goodness. He was a great believer in the ether – the invisible stuff that was supposed to fill all of space, but which does not exist.

Sadly, Maxwell died fairly young. Had he stuck around a bit longer he would have seen that his equations were right and lived to see the new waves that he had predicted. But at the time of his death many scientists didn't understand their importance.

Meanwhile, scientists continued to search for rays. In 1896 French scientist Antoine-Henri Becquerel (1852-1908) found strange rays coming off a chemical containing an element called uranium. Once again the rays were invisible but they did make photographic film go cloudy even when it was stored in the dark. So they probably ruined Becquerel's holiday snaps. Anyway, although Becquerel didn't know it at the time, he had discovered a vast new area of science: radioactivity. And a brilliant woman scientist was soon to probe its secrets. You can too – by reading her suffering story in the next chapter.

COURAGEOUS CURIE

Marie Curie had to leave her own country and learn a new language and endure starvation in order to get a science education. (And you thought your education was tough.) But that was the least of Marie's problems.

Horrible Science Hall of Fame: Marie Curie
(1867-1934) NATIONALITY: Polish/French

It was obvious that young Marie Sklodowska (as she was called before her marriage) was going to be a scientist when she grew up. Both her parents were teachers and young Marie was a clever girl who enjoyed reading science books. But there was a problem ... Marie was a girl and there were no places for girls in Polish universities in those days.

So Marie and her sister, Bronya, hatched an extraordinary plan...

SO, BRONYA, I GET A JOB AS A GOVERNESS AND YOU GO TO PARIS TO STUDY MEDICINE. I'LL SEND YOU MONEY.

And this is what the sisters did.

Marie's middle names ought to have been Stubborn, Dogged and Courageous. It took seven years of hard work and saving her meagre wages before she could attend the university in Paris. But when she got there she couldn't understand spoken French, and even with Bronya's help she was desperately poor. Often she had to choose between buying food or fuel to keep warm.

Most days she lived off bread and margarine and tea. Yet despite all these hardships she worked hard to improve her French and passed her exams with flying colours. But hold on a moment – why was it all such a struggle?

Why so tough for women?

If you've read this far you may have noticed that there seem to be very few women scientists. The problem was that many people (mostly men) thought that girls weren't up to learning science. In fact, these people (mostly men)

193

thought that females were stupid. Yes, I'm sorry girls, they really did think this. In 1879 French brain expert Gustav le Bon said:

There are a large number of women whose brains are closer in size to those of gorillas.

He added that a clever woman was as unusual as a gorilla with two heads.

A boring scientist says...

Scientists now know that the size of a person's brain is nothing to do with how clever they are.

But you can see why girls often never got the chance to learn about science. Women were shut out from many walks of life. For example, before the 1870s in the United States and the 1880s in Britain, women weren't allowed to train as doctors. Here's just one story to show how horribly unfair things were for wannabe women scientists.

The Fairfax family
Meet the Fairfax family:

Young Mary was a clever girl and she wanted to study science. But her mum and dad thought that girls could be driven mad by learning about maths and science. (Yes – they honestly did believe this, but it's not true so don't try this excuse, girls.) Instead, Mary was sent to boarding school where one lesson was how to stand up straight. The children were tortured by suits of iron hoops that kept their backs nice and straight.

Back home, Mary secretly taught herself maths after her parents went to bed. But her parents found out and took away her candles. Mary still wasn't put off. She lay awake in the dark and worked out maths problems in her head.

However, Mary didn't get the chance to write about science until her second husband gave her the books and encouragement she needed. (Her first husband had thought all women were stupid.)

Then, as Mary Somerville (1780-1872), she became a successful writer of bestselling science books on physics, astronomy and biology. So you see, most women had to battle to get a scientific education. And then they had to battle to get a scientific job.

So how about Marie Curie?

Marie was lucky – she got a job as a humble lab assistant. And in 1895 Marie married the boss of the science lab where she was working – Pierre Curie (1859-1906). The Curies worked together to make great discoveries in the field of radioactivity.

And if you don't know what that is, keep reading...

Suffering scientists fact file

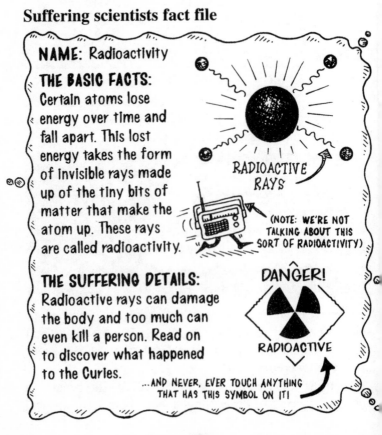

NAME: Radioactivity

THE BASIC FACTS:
Certain atoms lose energy over time and fall apart. This lost energy takes the form of invisible rays made up of the tiny bits of matter that make the atom up. These rays are called radioactivity.

RADIOACTIVE RAYS

(NOTE: WE'RE NOT TALKING ABOUT THIS SORT OF RADIOACTIVITY)

THE SUFFERING DETAILS:
Radioactive rays can damage the body and too much can even kill a person. Read on to discover what happened to the Curies.

DANGER!

RADIOACTIVE

...AND NEVER, EVER TOUCH ANYTHING THAT HAS THIS SYMBOL ON IT!

The Curies began by studying radioactivity in uranium, and they went on to find the same strange effect in another element, thorium. Next they turned their attention to an odd mystery...

Curies casebook

Here's what Marie's notes might have looked like. Well, perhaps. The notes were contaminated by radioactive chemicals and they've been locked away in a safe for years...

1896 – I've got a mystery on my hands. The chemical we're studying – pitchblende, a kind of mineral ore – is more radioactive than we thought given its known ingredient – uranium. I think there's a more radioactive substance called radium hidden in the pitchblende.

HOW TO MAKE RADIUM:

1 Get hold of lots of pitchblende. We can't afford to buy it but we did a deal with the mines to send us a rail wagon full of one tonne of waste pitchblende, the rubbish left after the uranium has been taken out. (There may be a few grams of radium hidden inside.)

2 Cart one tonne of waste pitchblende from the station to the lab.

3 Sift the pitchblende by hand to remove rubbish.

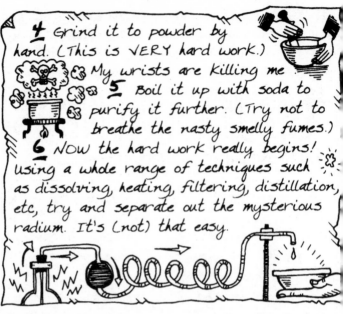

4 Grind it to powder by hand. (This is VERY hard work.) My wrists are killing me.

5 Boil it up with soda to purify it further. (Try not to breathe the nasty smelly fumes.)

6 NOW the hard work really begins! Using a whole range of techniques such as dissolving, heating, filtering, distillation, etc, try and separate out the mysterious radium. It's (not) that easy.

Especially as their lab was a grotty shed. (Check back to page 46 if you don't believe me.) Mind you, at least the Curies were happy. Marie Curie said:

It was in this miserable and cold shed that the best and happiest days of our life were spent.

She added that by the end of the day she was "broken with fatigue". Sounds even worse than double Science!

A glow of pride

One winter's night in 1898 Pierre and Marie visited their shed and saw a strange blue glow. It was made by radioactivity from the chemical radium – a totally unknown type of atom. The discovery made the Curies into

nstant celebrities and by the 1920s companies were quick
o cash in on the strange new chemical. Which of these
dverts seems too odd to be true?

THE RADIUM NEWS

Latest radium inventions!

1. RADIUM FACE POWDER & BEAUTY CREAMS
PUT THAT "GLOW" BACK INTO YOUR FACE!

2. RADIUM WATCH DIAL
GLOWS IN THE DARK
TELL THE TIME EVEN AT NIGHT

3. GLOW IN THE DARK FALSE TEETH!
NOW YOUR FRIENDS CAN APPRECIATE YOUR LOVELY SMILE EVEN AFTER DARK!

4. RADIUM GAS SPARKLETS
MAKES YOUR TONIC WATER GLOW IN THE DARK!
BREAKS THE ICE AT PARTIES

Answer: 4 All the other products were on sale. Which was a disaster because the radioactivity in radium made it really harmful. The watch dial workers fell ill after licking their radium coated paintbrushes.

Bet you never knew!
Oddly enough, radium can be used to kill diseased cells in people who are suffering from cancer, a range of diseases that cause body cells to multiply and form lumps. This discovery was made by Pierre Curie with the help of two doctors.

Two terrible tragedies

The Curies never faced up to the danger of radioactivity. Pierre carried some around in a test tube in his pocket and the radioactive rays burnt embarrassing holes in his trousers and made his legs sore.

Then in 1906 Pierre was killed – not by radium, however, but in a street accident. A heavy cart ran over him and squashed his head. But Marie died in 1934 of a blood disease called leukaemia, and the disease was probably caused by her exposure to radioactivity.

Bet you never knew!
Marie Curie received not one but two Nobel Prizes. She and Pierre won a 1903 prize for proving that radioactivity came from atoms and wasn't a chemical reaction as some other scientists thought. Then in 1911 Marie got a second prize for finding radium and polonium. (This was a second radioactive atom in the pitchblende.)

No wonder Marie Curie was the second most famous scientist of the twentieth century. Why only the second most famous? Well, the scientist in the next chapter was even more famous.

He was unbelievably famous...

AND YOU DON'T HAVE TO BE EINSTEIN TO WORK OUT WHO IT IS...

UNBELIEVABLE EINSTEIN

Albert Einstein is up there with Newton in the running for the greatest-scientist-of-all-time title. But what did he do to deserve such fame? Well, stop asking questions, read on and you'll find out...

Horrible Science Hall of Fame: Albert Einstein (1879-1955) NATIONALITY: German/Swiss/American

At the age of 12 young Albert announced:

I'll solve the riddles of the world.

He had decided to become a scientist. But Albert didn't do particularly well at school or college, remember? And in 1902 he found himself working as a lowly patent officer (someone who checks inventions to see if they will work) in Bern, Switzerland.

I'M PATENTLY UNSUITED FOR THIS WORK

But all the time he was dreaming of problems in science and in 1905 he shocked scientists with a series of brain-boggling discoveries...

Albert's brilliant breakthroughs

Albert published three main scientific articles. Any one of them deserved the Nobel Prize. Using complex mathematical calculations Albert showed...

PAPER 1

If you put a grain of pollen in water it seems to dance around. Water is made up of hydrogen and oxygen atoms which group together to form molecules. The movement of pollen is caused by these molecules bumping into it.

A boring historian says...

Remember the bit about water? (Check back to page 105 if you don't.) Well, although scientists believed in molecules they hadn't much proof that they existed! Einstein's paper provided the proof.

PAPER 2

Light is made up of tiny blips of energy called photons. It is possible to prove this through a mathematical study of the effects of light hitting metal.

A boring historian says...

Einstein was right again! Before this paper, scientists thought that light was made up of waves just as Maxwell had described them (see page 186). Einstein showed that light acts like a wave but it's actually made of these tiny blips of energy.

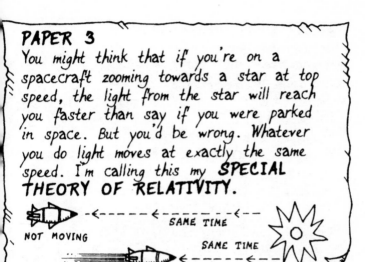

PAPER 3

You might think that if you're on a spacecraft zooming towards a star at top speed, the light from the star will reach you faster than say if you were parked in space. But you'd be wrong. Whatever you do light moves at exactly the same speed. I'm calling this my **SPECIAL THEORY OF RELATIVITY.**

NOT MOVING ← ← SAME TIME ← ←

MOVING ← ← SAME TIME ← ←

This sounds VERY odd. What Einstein was saying was that *nothing* can go faster than light and it doesn't matter what direction you're going in or how fast – light will always reach you at the same speed. But there were some even weirder results from his theory. They don't have much effect on Earth but meanwhile back in space...

Speedy quiz

Einstein's theory predicts some strange things that will happen to you as you approach the speed of light. Here they are, and just to make it more interesting we've added one effect that doesn't happen. Can you guess which one?

SCIENTISTS IN SPACE

SCIENCE OFFICER STELLAR   CAPTAIN COSMOS   SHIP'S CAT ORBIT

CONTINUED...

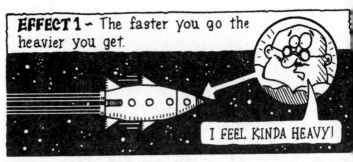

EFFECT 1 – The faster you go the heavier you get.

I FEEL KINDA HEAVY!

EFFECT 2 – The faster you go the shorter your space craft appears.

WE'RE GOING FLAT OUT!

EFFECT 3 – The faster you go the more colours in light change. For example, things that are red turn blue.

YOU'RE LOOKING A BIT OFF COLOUR, ORBIT!

EFFECT 4 – The faster you go the slower time passes.

THE SHIP'S CLOCKS HAVE SLOWED DOWN COMPARED TO THE CLOCKS ON EARTH.

WHAT A DRAG!

Answers: Effect 1 – TRUE. Einstein showed that the more energy a moving object has, the heavier it gets. Obviously the fast-moving starship and its crew have a lot of energy so their mass increases. At half the speed of light a 75 kg (166 lbs) scientist would be 12 kg (24 lbs) heavier! So it's a bad idea for people on a diet.

Effect 2 – TRUE. At half the speed of light the starship appears from the outside to be 13 per cent shorter.

Effect 3 – FALSE

Effect 4 – TRUE. The faster you go the slower time passes compared to time in a spaceship parked in space. You could go for a speedy trip in a spaceship and when you got back to Earth far more time would have passed. So when you land you find that you have travelled into the future!

Prove it!

These effects can be calculated using maths based on Einstein's theory. (Just don't ask me how – it's horribly complicated.) Now, you might think that you'd need to go impossibly fast to find out in practice if Einstein was right. But in fact, scientists already have the proof for the time-travel effect. No, don't get excited. Scientists have found that clocks on spacecraft speeding round the earth slow very slightly compared to clocks on the Earth. The time difference was only tiny fractions of a second – but it was enough to prove that Einstein was RIGHT!

In 1916, Albert followed this paper up with his General Theory of Relativity.

Teacher's tea-break teaser

This teaser really ought to be banned on the grounds that it is cruel to teachers. But if you really must do it, try it at the start of break on the grounds that it could take ages.

Tap lightly on the staff room door. When it opens, smile innocently and ask...

Answer: Well, it's a hard question. Your teacher can try but most teachers don't get very far and they can end up gibbering. If you're feeling kind you could help them out after the first 20 minutes or so. But to do that you'll have to read on...

Suffering scientists fact file

NAME: General Relativity

THE BASIC FACTS: Einstein thought about gravity and decided that it works like this: a really huge object like a planet or a star would curve space around it. If you want to imagine this just think what would happen if you dropped a cannon ball on your bed. Mind the cat now!

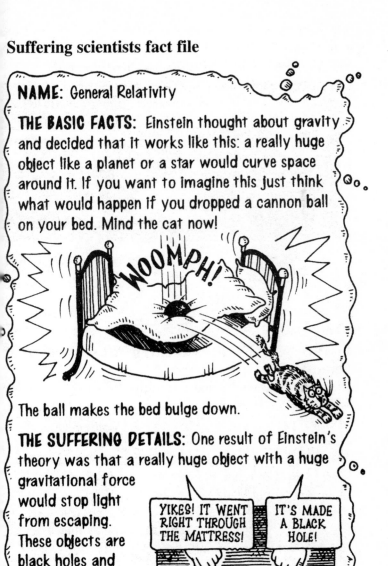

The ball makes the bed bulge down.

THE SUFFERING DETAILS: One result of Einstein's theory was that a really huge object with a huge gravitational force would stop light from escaping. These objects are black holes and they really do exist. (Turn back to page 91 if you don't believe me.)

YIKES! IT WENT RIGHT THROUGH THE MATTRESS!

IT'S MADE A BLACK HOLE!

Bet you never knew!
Einstein was an incredibly clever person, but he was useless at performing even the most basic tasks. He refused to wear socks and walked around the house in his bare feet. The scientist said there was no point in wearing socks because they only developed holes. Some historians have pointed out that this was because Einstein kept forgetting to cut his toe-nails.

I'M IMPRESSED!

Could you be an eccentric absent-minded scientist?

If you decided to become a scientist, how absent-minded would YOU be? Simply answer YES or NO to the following questions.

Have you ever...

1 fallen down a hole because you were thinking about science and not looking where you were going?

Note: According to one story, our old pal Thales of Miletus did this. He fell down a well because he was so busy thinking about astronomy. Well, well – fancy that! Luckily, the only thing that got hurt was his dignity.

2 forgotten to eat your supper because you were too busy doing your science homework?

Note: Lots of scientists did this including Isaac Newton and Archimedes (the ancient Greek scientist, remember?).

3 forgotten to take a bath for ages?

Archimedes did this too. Phfoar!

4 spent ages in the bathroom when your parents forced you to have a bath, because you were doing scientific experiments with the soap and the rubber duck?

Note: When Archimedes got really smelly he was carried to the bath house where his slaves bathed him. But all the time he was trying to draw scientific diagrams using the bath oil.

5 left your friends waiting for hours whilst you got on with your science homework.

Note: Newton did this when he was at College. He simply forgot his friends were waiting in the next room. After a while he didn't have any friends.

6 used a cheque that you got from your granny for a birthday present as a bookmark and forgotten to pay it into the bank?

Note: Einstein did this one day in the early 1920s and the cheque was for lots of money.

7 got off your bike at the bottom of a steep hill and then forgotten to get back on it. So you walked the rest of the journey because you were thinking about science?

Note: Newton did this as a young man when he travelled to market. Only instead of a bike he had a horse.

8 forgotten where your house is?

Note: Einstein did this when he moved to America in the 1930s. He had to phone up the secretary of the college where he worked to ask for directions.

How did you get on? Give yourself one mark for each YES answer.

What your score means:

0 to **3**: You are perfectly normal.

4 to **6**: You are a bit absent-minded but there's nothing to worry about.

6 to **9**: You are definitely an absent-minded scientist. Oh well, don't ever change – you might win the Nobel Prize one day.

Einstein's errors

Einstein was so clever that some people think that he never got anything wrong. Well, for all of us ordinary folk, it'll come as a great relief to know that amazing Albert made some whopping blunders. He admitted, for example, that his biggest mistake was not realizing that the universe is growing bigger.

A boring scientist says...

Remember Hubble and his discovery that space was getting bigger as a result of the Big Bang? Einstein's calculations for General Relativity showed this result but he refused to believe it and only admitted he was wrong after meeting Hubble in 1930. But Einstein made an even worse error.

Einstein's end

There are four forces in the universe: gravity, electromagnetism and two forces that operate inside atoms. Albert reckoned that he could come up with a single theory to explain gravity and electromagnetism.

He failed.

But he spent his last 30 years working on complex but ultimately fruitless sums. It's a bit like you being stuck in an endless maths lesson struggling with impossible questions. (What'ya mean every maths lesson seems like that?) And when he died there was a set of uncompleted calculations by his bedside.

Bet you never knew!
In 1933 a new political party came into power in Germany. They were called the Nazis. The Nazis hated Jews and it so happened that Einstein's family were Jewish. Einstein was forced to flee to America. And he was just one of many. During the 1930s scores of German scientists, many of them from Jewish families, fled Nazi Germany. And then things got far worse. Read on to find out what happened next...

BRILLIANT BOHR

In 1940 and 1941 the Germans conquered most of Europe and many more scientists found themselves in danger. They included a brilliant Danish physicist named Niels Bohr.

Horrible Science Hall of Fame: Niels Bohr (1885-1962) NATIONALITY: Danish

Young Niels was a big tough lad who talked rather slowly. Kids at his school thought he was rather thick, especially as he was always getting into fights. (That's not a very smart thing to do.) But Niels *was* clever, especially at science. And it was a pity that the big, clumsy lad was always smashing test-tubes and blowing up chemicals in the science lab. Here's what his teacher said:

BOOM!

Oh that must be Bohr!

Niels went to university to study physics and he soon became well-known in college for his brilliance. He was so clever he corrected mistakes in his textbooks and was so wrapped up in science that when he played in goal in football he wrote scientific calculations on the goalposts. Then he made daring saves at the last moment.

Not surprisingly for such a thoughtful scientist, Niels got interested in the biggest discovery of the early twentieth century: quantum mechanics.

Suffering scientists fact file

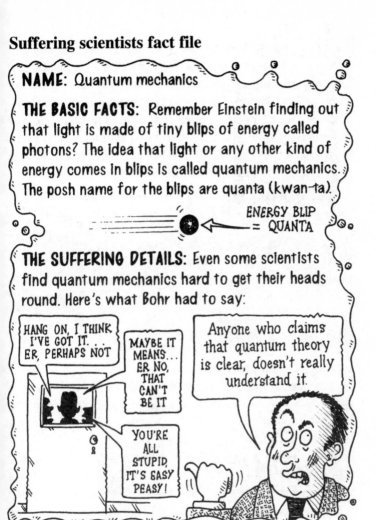

NAME: Quantum mechanics

THE BASIC FACTS: Remember Einstein finding out that light is made of tiny blips of energy called photons? The idea that light or any other kind of energy comes in blips is called quantum mechanics. The posh name for the blips are quanta (kwan-ta).

ENERGY BLIP = QUANTA

THE SUFFERING DETAILS: Even some scientists find quantum mechanics hard to get their heads round. Here's what Bohr had to say:

HANG ON, I THINK I'VE GOT IT. . . ER, PERHAPS NOT

MAYBE IT MEANS... ER NO, THAT CAN'T BE IT

YOU'RE ALL STUPID, IT'S EASY PEASY!

Anyone who claims that quantum theory is clear, doesn't really understand it.

Bohr's breakthroughs

In 1913 Bohr was working in England with Ernest Rutherford (1871-1937), the New Zealand-born British scientist who used experiments to develop the idea of an atom as a solid centre surrounded by electrons. Well, Bohr worked out how the electrons were arranged in atoms, and how they each had a particular amount of energy.

Bohr spent the rest of his working life developing the ideas of quantum mechanics. He ran a research institute in Copenhagen and organized conferences where scientists from all over Europe argued about the make-up of atoms. Once, these arguments got so fierce that German scientist Werner Heisenberg (1901-1976) burst into tears, and often Bohr got so cross that he rushed out of the room and started weeding the garden to let off steam.

Going down a bomb

In the late 1930s, using maths, Bohr showed that by splitting an atom in two you could release energy in the form of radioactivity. In 1939 rumours began to circulate that German scientist Otto Hahn (1879-1968) had actually succeeded in splitting an atom of uranium. Bohr knew that by splitting billions of atoms at once you could release huge amounts of energy. This could make a terrible bomb with the power to wipe out cities. Such a weapon would make the Nazis masters of the world.

On a trip to the USA, Bohr warned Einstein what was going on and Einstein warned the President. President Roosevelt decided that the USA should make its own atom bomb. But then Bohr made a dangerous mistake. He went back to Denmark. Within months the entire country was taken over by the Germans and Bohr found himself in terrible danger.

Run for your life!

If Bohr had been able to write to his friend Einstein during those dark days his letters might have looked like this...

Copenhagen, September 1943

Dear Albert

I'm in danger. I suppose it's my fault but I can't stand these Nazis who have occupied my country and forced so many of my scientist pals to flee Germany. So I refused to help them. In fact don't tell anyone, but I've been sending secret letters to English scientists telling them what little I know about German atom bomb plans. (It's on the cards, but it's a few years off.) If the Germans find out I'll be shot as a spy. Yours, Niels

A safe house, somewhere in Denmark
September 1943

Dear Albert
A friend of mine in the Danish Resistance tipped me off. They told me that the Germans were going to arrest me tomorrow. I had to go into hiding. But Albert, I'm really, really scared. Patrols of soldiers are knocking on every door. My Resistance friends have a plan to get me out of the country. We go tonight – it's now or never. Is this goodbye?
Niels

215

A fishing boat,
Somewhere between Denmark and Sweden,
September 1943

Dear Albert

Tonight I hid in the back of the car as we drove towards the coast. Then I crawled on my hands and knees across a muddy field towards the beach. I was expecting a searchlight to pin-point me in the dark, a shouted warning, the sound of gunfire.

Nothing happened!

Next I had to wade into the icy waves to reach this fishing boat. Now I'm at sea – tired and cold and wet. At any moment I'm expecting to see a German patrol boat looming through the darkness.

They're out there, I know, looking for me.

Glad you're not here.

Niels

A safe house in Sweden, September 1943

German
← Spies

Dear Albert

I'm still in danger. German spies know I'm in the country and my British friends here say the Germans have orders to kill me on sight. I've heard the British government has sent a plane to fetch me to England. But it could be too late. I'll write soon ... if I live.

Niels

The bomb bay, A mosquito bomber, Somewhere over the North Sea

Dear Albert

I am dying. No, I haven't been shot, even though the German agents tailed me to the airfield and we only just took off in time. No, I'm dying of cold in this plane. It's so cold in this bomb bay and there isn't enough fresh air to breath. I banged on the sides but the crew can't hear me. And if the German fighters catch us I will have a hot fiery death instead of a cold frozen one. I should never have become a scientist. I can't stay awake ...
    I'm falling asleep. If I sleep, I die. Goodbye old friend.
    Niels

A happy ending

Niels Bohr survived the flight – just. When the plane landed in England he was unconscious from the cold and lack of air. From England, Bohr travelled on to the USA where he found out about the American plans to build an atom bomb. Bohr was shocked by the scheme and he was appalled when two atom bombs were used to end the war with Japan in August 1945. He spent the rest of his life campaigning for the peaceful use of the atom's power and the sharing of scientific information.

MODERN FREAKY PHYSICISTS

If you like to think about really deep questions then you'll definitely want to be a physicist when you grow up. Since the days of Einstein and Bohr physicists have found out an unbelievable amount about atoms and the universe.

Starting in the 1940s scientists in Britain and the USA began to smash atoms to pieces using machines called particle accelerators that use powerful magnetic forces to make bits of atom move at incredible speeds before smashing into more atoms. The scientists found a bewildering range of tiny bits (or particles as they called them) were given off by these impacts.

The particles were classified and sorted out by US scientist Murray Gell-Mann in 1964. Gell-Mann used advanced maths to calculate that the basic building blocks for the nucleus of atoms were even more tiny particles called quarks (kwar-ks). These were held together with smaller particles called gluons (gloo-ons). It's an amazingly strange world.

Dare you discover ... how gluons work?

All you need is...
A football and friend

All you do is...
1 You and your friend must toss the ball to and fro between you. When you catch the ball, instantly throw it back.
2 Whatever happens you must not drop the ball. If you do you must each move a big step closer together.

What do you notice...
a) We feel as if we are being glued together by the ball.
b) We kept dropping the ball and ended up with our noses touching.

) We felt drawn together by a strange force even though either of us dropped the ball.

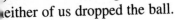

Answer: a) The ball is like the gluons. Although it is not actually sticking you together it is hard to move apart whilst you are playing the game.

Bet you never knew!

Murray Gell-Mann was so clever that when he went to a special school for clever children he found the lessons dull because they were not hard enough, and he didn't enjoy physics. He went to university at the age of 15 and only got interested in the subject at that stage.

The big questions

Meanwhile, other scientists have been puzzling over whether there is a single theory that explains all the forces in the universe. Remember Einstein and how he to tried to explain gravity and electromagnetism? Well, scientists now know that there are two more forces to consider, both operating inside atoms.

Suffering scientists fact file

NAME: Forces inside atoms

THE BASIC FACTS: The two forces are...

1 The weak nuclear force:
Studied mathematically by Italian scientist Enrico Fermi (1901-54) in 1934, this force makes atoms give out radioactive particles.

2 The strong nuclear force:
This force holds the particles that make up the centre of the atom together. It was first outlined in maths calculations in 1935 by Japanese scientist Hideki Yukawa (1907-1981).

FORCE 1: MAKES ATOMS GIVE OUT RADIOACTIVE PARTICLES

FORCE 2: HOLDS THESE PARTICLES TOGETHER

THE SUFFERING DETAILS: Both forces have since been proven by experiments. The strong force is 100,000,000 (100 million) times stronger than the weak force. That's strength for you!

But physicists aren't yet satisfied. For them the ultimate goal is something more than a TOE or a GUT. A what?

Suffering expressions

IT'S NOT WORKING!

IS IT YOUR **TOE** OR **GUT**?

Should you call a doctor?

Answer:

No. A TOE is a Theory Of Everything and a GUT is a
Grand Unified Theory. They mean the same thing: a
explanation of the electro-magnetic force (that's electrici
and magnetism, remember) and the two forces inside th
atom in a single set of mathematical equations. A t
order? You bet. But physicists won't be satisfied un
they've also fitted gravity into their TOEs and GUTs.

■nstein spent years looking for this theory and at present
  any physicists including Stephen Hawking (see page 92)
  ▪e working to find it too. No one quite knows exactly what
  will be like, but in 1984 British physicist Michael Green
  nd American John Schwarz suggested that their
  alculations could include all the forces by imagining
  ▪articles not as dots but as superstrings – tiny string-like
  ɔops.

It all sounds very weird doesn't it? But you might also
think it's fascinating in its strangeness. Perhaps you *will*
decide to become a physicist. After all, just imagine that
you're the person who finally finds the TOE? The Nobel
Prize is a dead cert and you'd become incredibly famous
and be remembered as one of the greatest scientists ever.

But wait a minute – it's not that easy. What about all the
scientists who went before you? And look at how many of
them encountered hardship and difficulties and even death.
So here's the BIG QUESTION. Do you really want to
become a scientist? I mean, is it worth all that *suffering*?

ERK! ... I'M
NOT SURE – I'D
BETTER READ
THE LAST CHAPTER

EPILOGUE

Well, for starters, just be glad that other people prepared to suffer for science. Where would you be if the weren't? Just read on and find out...

A different world

You walk out of the school gates. It's the end of anoth hard day and you're feeling rather worn out. So worn o that you don't notice that you've just walked into *alternative universe*.

There's something odd about the street. There are n cars, only horse-drawn carts. But there is no one to colle you and after waiting ages for a bus you walk the te kilometres home.

Your house is in darkness except for oil lamps, and when you ask where the TV is your dad looks puzzled.

The TV and video have vanished, along with the fridge, the microwave and the CD player.

Then your mum comes in and asks how your alchemy class went and whether you learnt any good spells.

And now it's your turn to look puzzled.

You're starving and ask your mum about tea.

"Yes dear," says your mum. "It's your favourite – some delicious oatmeal gruel."

You consider saying something about jelly but then

ink better of it. Your parents are clearly quite mad. The
uel is as bad as it looks, and then you go to bed. You
rush your teeth with water and splash a little on your face
ecause the toothpaste and soap seems to have vanished
om the bathroom along with the loo cleaner, the bubble
ath and the rubber duck. A cold bed with itchy, coarsely
oven sheets awaits. Your radio-controlled plane and
attery-operated space-shuttle model have been replaced
y a wooden doll and an iron hoop.

It's morning. You open your eyes and look about your
room. It's almost bare except for the hard crudely-carved
wooden furniture. So it wasn't a nightmare. This is really
happening. And you're sure it's real – once you taste your
morning gruel. Once again you set off to walk to school –
and you think. Think about where you are and what is
happening. Oh well, science again today.

Science.

So that's what it's all about. You realize your mum had
called it "alchemy". That's it, you've stumbled into a world
where science never existed. A world where technology –
electricity and jelly and toothpaste and TV and cars and
comfortable beds – just don't exist. And they don't exist
because the scientists who made the discoveries that made
the technology possible never existed either. No Faraday,
so no electricity. No plastics or radios or ANYTHING!

And as you walk through the school gates you pray that
at least your school will be normal again. You never

thought you'd be so desperate to go into a science lesso You're thinking so hard that you walk through the shimmering opening back into your old universe witho even noticing. Until you look back and see the cars an buses and the usual street scene. You're saved. Saved b science!

Of course, without the discoveries made by science li would be miserable. But scientists didn't go into scienc just to make life more comfortable for the rest of us. N there's one BIG reason why people become scientists. It a feeling shared by every scientist in this book. It's becaus they think that science is fascinating. And even when it' horrible, it's horribly fascinating, amazing and eve exciting. And although science lessons can be boring – rea science is never boring.

Take French scientist Michel Chevreul (1786-1889). He worked on animal fats and in 1823 found that they can be separated into other chemicals. He died when he was 103 but although he never retired, he never got bored of scienc either. And at the age of 90 he began to study the effects o ageing.

So what about you. Do you *really* want to be a scientist? Well, whatever you decide, just remember one thing. Yes – science *can* be horrible, but it's worth all the suffering just to be a scientist.

And that's the horrible truth!